Law Essentials

PUBLIC LAW

Law Essentials

PUBLIC LAW

Jean McFadden, M.A., LL.B.

Visiting Lecturer in Law, University of Strathclyde and Glasgow City Councillor

and

Dale McFadzean, B.A. (Hons). F.H.E.A.

Programme Leader for Law, University of Paisley

DUNDEE UNIVERSITY PRESS
2007

First published in Great Britain in 2007 by
Dundee University Press
University of Dundee
Dundee DD1 4HN

www.dundee.ac.uk/dup

ISBN 978-1-84586-031-8

No natural forests were destroyed to make this product;
only farmed timber was used and replanted.

British Library Cataloguing-in-Publication Data
A catalogue record for this book is available on request from the British Library

Typeset by Waverley Typesetters, Fakenham
Printed and bound by Bell & Bain Ltd, Glasgow

CONTENTS

TABLE OF CASES

TABLE OF STATUTES

TABLE OF CONVENTIONS

1 INTRODUCTION

Scots law deals with many specific subject areas, such as criminal law, administrative law and the law of delict, among others. Each of these areas is known as a "branch" of law. For simplicity, each of these branches is further categorised into two distinct groupings: public law and private law. There is no real technical reason for these groupings. They are simply a useful way of categorising the various branches of law under separate headings. This book is concerned with the branch known as public law and a useful starting point is to define what this branch signifies.

With "public law", the involvement of the State is paramount. Public law relates to the operation of government and the regulation of the relationship between government and citizens. It also regulates other public bodies, such as the courts, the Scottish Parliament, local government and even the police. Public law is usually considered to embrace two major branches of law: constitutional law and administrative law. The scope of this book will concentrate on constitutional law. For those readers who require an outline of administrative law it is suggested that they read *Scottish Administrative Law Essentials* by the same authors.

There is no hard and fast definition of "constitutional law". It is suggested that it covers those laws which regulate the structure and functions of the principal organs of government and their relationship to each other and to the citizen. There is also no hard and fast demarcation in the United Kingdom between constitutional law and other branches of the law. For example, family law raises questions about the protection of family life (involving consideration of the European Convention on Human Rights), and labour law may raise concerns about freedom of association and picketing – all matters of constitutional importance.

As such, public law is a large and complicated subject which naturally involves a consideration of not only the relevant law but also the political and historical contexts within which the law operates. The aim of this book is not to provide a definitive exposition of public law in the UK. Instead, it intends to cover some of the most important aspects of the law in a manner which will hopefully facilitate ease of learning. To this end, we have included a glossary of basic public law terms to assist the novice reader.

BASIC GLOSSARY

- *The principal organs of government*: The legislature, the executive and the judiciary
- *Legislature*: This is the law-making body in any state. In the UK it consists of "the Queen in Parliament" (and those bodies to which the Queen in Parliament has devolved legislative power). "The Queen in Parliament" means the House of Commons, the House of Lords and the monarch (queen or king).
- *Executive*: This is the body responsible for the formulation of policy. It is also the body responsible for the carrying into effect of the laws made by the legislature. In law, the monarch is the head of the executive, but the real power lies with the Prime Minister and the Cabinet. So the executive is the Government, ie the Prime Minister and all the other Ministers (not all of whom are in the Cabinet), the Scottish Executive and the Welsh Ministers.
- *Judiciary*: This is the body responsible for settling legal disputes and for interpreting and applying the law. It consists of the judges sitting in the Queen's courts. In our system the judiciary is said to be independent of the legislature and the executive and this independence is a constitutional value of the highest importance.
- *Statute law*: The body of principles and rules of law laid down in statutes (ie Acts of Parliament and Acts of the Scottish Parliament), statutory instruments, Scottish statutory instruments and statutory instruments of the National Assembly for Wales, as distinct from UK common law. Statute law is a superior form of law in that it can amend or overrule any inconsistent principle or rule of law found elsewhere (in common law or books or custom and practice), even those of the Scottish Parliament.
- *Common law*: This refers to judge-made law. It consists of the body of principles and rules of law stated by judges in their opinions delivered on deciding various disputes or claims, or derived inductively from the examination of various opinions in various relevant cases.
- *[Royal] Prerogative powers*: These are common law powers which the monarch can exercise on his authority. In practice, most of these powers are exercised only on the advice and authority of Government Ministers. Prerogative powers are not derived from statute, since they are common law, but they can be modified or abolished by statute and can fall into disuse. The courts also have a role in determining the existence, scope and proper use of prerogative powers.

- *Constitutional monarchy*: This means a monarchy whose power is limited and can be exercised only according to the laws, customs and conventions of the constitution. The king or queen may reign but all significant acts of government are carried out on the advice of Ministers who are responsible to Parliament, or are actually carried out by the Ministers themselves in the name of the monarch. The monarch should be politically neutral and refrain from becoming involved in political controversy.

- *Conventions*: These are rules of constitutional behaviour or political practice which are looked upon as binding by those whom they concern. They are not laid down either by statute or by common law. The courts will not enforce them, although they recognise their existence. For example, the Queen normally invites the leader of the party with the largest number of seats to form a Government.

- *Federal system (of government)*: In a federal system, the powers of government are divided between the general or central government on the one hand and the regional or State governments on the other. The USA and Germany are two well-known examples.

- *Unitary system (of government)*: There is one legislature or Parliament for the entire country and it is the supreme law-making body. The powers of any local, regional or sub-national legislatures which may exist are limited by and subordinate to the supreme legislature. This is the system we have in the UK. The Westminster Parliament had the power to prorogue (and eventually abolish) the Northern Ireland Parliament, as it has with the Scottish Parliament, the Northern Ireland Assembly or the National Assembly for Wales.

- *Devolution*: This means that a superior body grants powers to an inferior body and has the power to override action taken by that inferior body, even within the range of the powers devolved. By legislative devolution, central government confers on an inferior body, in addition, the powers to make laws on matters which are specifically transferred to it, as with the Scottish Parliament.

2 THE UNITED KINGDOM CONSTITUTION

A constitution embodies the rules which govern the structure and functions of government and the relationship between the State and its citizens. Most countries have a "narrow" constitution, consisting of a written document with a special legal status which sets out the framework and principal functions of government and the principles by which the organs of government operate. Such constitutions normally have a higher status than other laws and can be amended only by a special process different from that by which ordinary law is changed. There is often a special constitutional court which applies and interprets a narrow constitution, such as the Supreme Court in the USA, or the Federal Constitutional Court in Germany.

The United Kingdom does not have a constitution in this narrow sense, since there is no single document from which the organs of government derive their authority. Instead, the UK has a "broad" constitution, consisting of a collection of legal and non-legal rules found to varying degrees in Acts of Parliament, case law and political practices and procedures. The disparate nature of these sources often leads to the UK constitution being described as "unwritten". However, this is inaccurate and it is best to describe the constitution as uncodified, partly written or evolutionary.

GENERAL CHARACTERISTICS

As well as being uncodified, the UK constitution is also a unitary one, in that it is characterised by a single sovereign legislature and a centralised government. It does not, however, subscribe to a strict unitary model, and varying degrees of power have been devolved through the establishment of a Scottish Parliament, a Welsh Assembly and a Northern Irish Assembly. Many critics believe that a written constitution, in the narrow sense, coupled with a Bill of Rights, should be adopted in the UK. This would make the constitutional rights of citizens clearer and more easily accessible. This line of reasoning has been fuelled in recent years by our accession to the European Union, and our incorporation of the European Convention on Human Rights (EHCR) by virtue of the Human Rights Act 1998.

The existence of parliamentary sovereignty combined with the dominant position which the executive occupies in relation to the legislature as a result of, among other things, the party system and the "first-past-the-post" electoral system, has meant that governments are generally able to ensure parliamentary support for the implementation of their policies. More particularly, as a consequence of the doctrine of parliamentary sovereignty itself, the courts have no power to challenge the validity of legislation and no distinctive procedures for amending the law of the constitution are recognised.

Although the constitution has evolved over the centuries with few major changes, its development cannot be fully understood without some knowledge of the historical processes which have helped to shape it. In part because of the overriding power of Parliament and in part because of the pliability of many constitutional conventions, the constitution has proved itself flexible and adaptable in the face of changing circumstances. Furthermore, it exhibits the principle of the parliamentary executive and that of the constitutional monarchy whereby, under the influence of convention, the Sovereign's functions are normally of very little political significance.

WHERE TO FIND PUBLIC LAW

Legislation

There are many sources of public law in the UK. The first of these is Acts of Parliament or statute law. Acts of constitutional significance are not subject to any special status and are passed using the normal legislative procedure. Important examples of public law statutes include:

- the Bill of Rights 1688 and the Claim of Right 1689 which laid out the foundations of parliamentary supremacy and the rejection of rule by prerogative right;
- the Acts of Union 1706 and 1707 which created the Parliament of Great Britain;
- the European Communities Act 1972, providing for the incorporation of European Community law into the domestic law of the United Kingdom;
- the Scotland Act 1998 which re-established the Scottish Parliament; and
- the Human Rights Act 1998 which incorporates ECHR into domestic law.

The peculiar importance attached in the UK to legislation flows from the relationship between the legislature and the judiciary, ie between

Parliament and the courts. As a result of the doctrine of parliamentary sovereignty, the courts in Britain have no power to pronounce on the validity of legislation which has been properly enacted by Parliament (*British Railways Board* v *Pickin* (1974); *Jackson* v *Attorney-General* (2005)). In contrast, the United States Supreme Court has long possessed the power of judicial review, and can declare Acts of Congress and of the President to be unconstitutional. The British courts can interpret a statute but they cannot strike it down as being invalid. It is open to the UK Parliament at any time to alter the law, both statute law and judge-made law and, in this way, the UK Parliament always has the last word.

Even in light of modern legislation such as the Human Rights Act 1998, the final say still lies with Parliament. The 1998 Act places an obligation on the courts to give effect to all legislation consistently with the Convention rights. Where this is not possible, certain higher courts may issue a declaration of incompatibility under s 4 of the 1998 Act. It must be noted, however, that this provision does not affect the sovereignty of Parliament and the issuing of such a declaration does not affect the validity, continuing operation or enforcement of any offending laws. Ultimately, Parliament must legislate to avoid any incompatibility with Convention rights. An example of this can be found in the case of *A (and Others)* v *Secretary of State for the Home Department* (2004) where the House of Lords held that the powers of the Secretary of State under Part 4 of the Anti-Terrorism, Crime and Security Act 2001 (ATCSA) were incompatible with Arts 5 and 14 of the ECHR relating to the right to liberty and the right to freedom from discrimination. The ruling was accepted by the Government and the Part 4 powers under the ATCSA were repealed and replaced with a system of non-discriminatory control orders under the Prevention of Terrorism Act 2005.

Common law (case law)

The second source is common law or case law. This falls into two categories: (i) the common law proper; and (ii) statutory interpretation.

The common law proper

This consists of the laws and customs which have been declared to be law by judges in decisions in particular cases coming before them. For example, in *Entick* v *Carrington* (1765) it was held that a Secretary of State had no power to issue general warrants for the arrest and search of those publishing seditious documents.

Statutory interpretation

Important issues of public law may also arise from the courts' interpretation of statutes. For example, in *Fox* v *Stirk* (1970), the court interpreted the meaning of "resident" in the Representation of the People Act 1949 as encompassing students living in a college or hall of residence, thus enabling them to vote in that constituency rather than the one where their home was.

European Community law

This became a source of public law when the UK joined the EEC in 1973 after the passing of the European Communities Act 1972. By virtue of the 1972 Act, the courts have to apply EC (or Community) law as part of the domestic law of the United Kingdom. The role of European Community law is complex and worthy of a discussion in its own right; however, the two important points to be made for the purposes of this discussion are:

   (i) the overriding principle of Community law is the primacy of it. This means that where a national law is in conflict with it, Community law prevails; and

   (ii) Community law can and often does confer rights and impose obligations on individual people in the Member States, and these rights and obligations are enforceable in the national courts.

The law and custom of Parliament

Parliament regulates its own procedures and a body of law and custom has developed throughout the centuries of Parliament's existence. These rules are contained largely in Standing Orders, resolutions passed by either the House of Commons or the House of Lords, and in rulings by the Speaker of the House of Commons. Examples include the arrangement of business behind the Speaker's chair, the Speaker's duty to protect minorities, the functions of the Leaders of the two Houses, and the allocation of time to the Opposition. Generally, the ordinary courts have no jurisdiction to apply and enforce the law and custom of Parliament.

Authoritative writers

Where there are no relevant statutory or case authorities, the judiciary may consult "books of authority". These include writings, books and articles not only by leading public lawyers, but also by historians and political scientists. They are not legally binding and examples include A V Dicey's *Study of the Law of the Constitution* (1885) and *Constitutional and Administrative Law* (1971), now in its 13th edition by Bradley and Ewing (formerly Wade and Bradley).

Conventions

The term "conventions" is used to denote rules of political behaviour which are regarded as binding by those whom they concern but which would not be enforced in the courts if the matter were to be brought before them. Conventions evolve over a period of time and are followed through political self-interest, since damaging repercussions would ensue on any breach. There are many examples to be found, including:

(i) in law, the Queen may refuse to give the Royal Assent to a Bill. By convention, she does not do so but acts on the advice of the Prime Minister;

(ii) the House of Commons will not allow the House of Lords to amend any financial provision in a Bill without the House of Commons' consent; and

(iii) the Cabinet and office of the Prime Minister are based purely on convention and are not established by Act of Parliament.

Conventions are not unique to the UK constitution and are found in the constitutions of most democratic countries. For example, the United States President is, in constitutional terms, chosen by electoral colleges but, largely by convention, he is directly elected.

Essential Facts

- The UK constitution is uncodified, ie not found in a single written document. It is a unitary constitution featuring devolution and a constitutional monarchy.
- The constitution of the UK can be found in a number of key sources: Acts of Parliament; common law; European Community law; conventions; the law and custom of Parliament; and authoritative writings.
- The sovereignty of Parliament means that the UK Parliament has no *legal* restrictions on what laws it can pass.

- The UK courts can interpret a statute but they cannot strike it down as being invalid. It is open to the UK Parliament at any time to alter the law, both statute law and judge-made law, and, in this way, the UK Parliament always has the last word.

Essential Cases

British Railways Board v Pickin (1974): if errors in the procedure of passing a Bill have occurred, it is for Parliament alone to correct them. The court cannot question the validity of any Act of Parliament.

A (and Others) v Secretary of State for the Home Department (2004): example of a declaration of incompatibility eliciting legislative change by Parliament.

3 DOCTRINES OF THE CONSTITUTION

In order fully to understand the workings of contemporary constitutional law, one must also be aware of the fundamental doctrines of the United Kingdom constitution. These doctrines are the embodiment of many years of constitutional history and lend explanatory significance to many of the concepts contained within public law. Therefore, the purpose of this chapter is to give the reader an overview of the key doctrines of the UK constitution.

SEPARATION OF POWERS

The classic exposition of the Separation of Powers is that of Montesquieu:

> "When the legislative and executive powers are united in the same person, or in the same body of magistrates, there can be no liberty ... Again, there is no liberty if the power of judging is not separated from the legislative and executive. If it were joined with the legislative, the life and liberty of the subject would be exposed to arbitrary control; for the judge would then be the legislator. If it were joined to the executive power, the judge might behave with violence and oppression. There would be an end to everything, if the same man, or the same body, whether of the nobles or of the people, were to exercise those three powers, that of enacting laws, that of executing public affairs, and that of trying crimes or individual causes."
> (*The Spirit of the Laws* (1748))

The doctrine of the Separation of Powers recognises three separate organs of government, namely the legislature, the executive and the judiciary. In the UK, the legislature is represented by the UK Parliament and devolved institutions, the executive by Government in the development and administration of policy, and the judiciary by judges who settle disputes and interpret the law. Each organ should be vested with one main function of government only and should not interfere with the functions of another. It is debatable, however, to what extent this separation truly exists in the UK.

Membership overlap

Legislature and executive

A complete separation of powers would mean that there should be no Ministers in Parliament; but, by convention, UK Government Ministers should be members either of the House of Commons or of the House of Lords. This in turn makes them accountable and responsible to Parliament. There is, however, a statutory limit placed upon the number of Ministers who may sit and vote as members of the House of Commons. That number is currently limited to 95 Ministers, by virtue of s 2 of the House of Commons Disqualification Act 1975. That same Act disqualifies many categories of office-holders from membership of the House of Commons, such as civil servants, police and members of the armed forces. Many civil servants, and the police, are also forbidden to take part in political activities, thus the separation of the legislature and the executive is quite strict and it is only Ministers who hold a dual role. The same can be said of the devolved institutions within the UK.

Judiciary and legislature

There is membership overlap in the House of Lords, since the Law Lords (for the time being, until the provisions of the Constitutional Reform Act 2005 come fully into force) are judges and members of the legislature. But all other full-time judicial appointments disqualify from membership of the House of Commons. This is also true of the devolved institutions in the UK.

Judiciary and executive

Prior to the introduction of the 2005 Act, the Lord Chancellor was head of the judiciary and was entitled to preside over the House of Lords which is the final court of appeal in the UK. However, the Lord Chancellor is no longer a judge or head of the judiciary, though he continues to have responsibility for the judiciary and the courts system. He is also a member of the UK Cabinet and a supporter of the political party in power.

Control

The executive controls the legislature to a large extent. This is mainly because of the strong governments returned by the "first-past-the-post" electoral system, the strong party whip system, and the Prime Minister's powers of patronage.

Executive and judiciary

There is a strict separation here and the separation and independence of the judiciary is assured by various means:

(a) Judges are paid a fixed, annual salary which is not dependent on an annual vote in the House of Commons, and is charged to the

Consolidated Fund. Parliament is asked to approve increases every so often, and cannot reduce the salaries.

(b) Judges hold office *ad vitam aut culpam*, ie for life and during good behaviour.

(c) Judges are protected from actions of defamation by the law of privilege, ensuring that they can speak freely in judgment.

Judiciary and legislature

The vast majority of judges are ineligible to be elected. In addition, English judges can only be removed from office by addresses from both Houses of Parliament, and indeed there has been only one example of this since 1700 (Jonah Barrington, an Irish judge, was removed in 1830). According to the doctrine of parliamentary sovereignty, the UK Parliament can, by passing legislation, nullify judicial decisions both prospectively and retrospectively. So, in that sense, the judiciary is subordinate to the legislature.

Exercise of functions

Executive and legislature

Ministers (ie the executive) have legislative powers in that they may make delegated legislation, for example statutory instruments. An especial concern in this respect has been the controversially increasing use of "Henry VIII" clauses by Ministers.

Executive and judiciary

Essential judicial functions, such as the conduct of civil and criminal trials, are dealt with by the judiciary. However, many disputes are dealt with by tribunals which are staffed by people who are not judges, and who are appointed by the executive. These tribunals are exercising judicial functions, though in a less formal way than the court. Some matters are also dealt with by means of a public inquiry in which a reporter, appointed by the executive, or a Minister makes a decision in line with departmental policy, after hearing all the relevant arguments.

Judiciary and legislature

Each House of Parliament has the power to enforce its own privileges and to punish those who offend them, ie acting as judge of a Member's conduct. In declaring and interpreting the law, the judges are making law, either in areas of the common law or in statutory interpretation. Judicial decisions are an important source of law in areas of police powers, civil liberties and administrative law.

Position of the Lord Chancellor

Prior to June 2003, the Lord Chancellor was a member of the executive and had a seat in the Cabinet. He was also a member of the legislature, being Speaker of the House of Lords and also having a seat in the Lords. Furthermore, he was also head of the judiciary in England and Wales, a member of the House of Lords Appellate Committee and a member of the Judicial Committee of the Privy Council. The Lord Chancellor's Department was also responsible for recommending individuals for appointment as judges in England and Wales. As a member of the Cabinet, the Lord Chancellor could not be politically impartial nor could he be impartial in his role as a government spokesman in the House of Lords. Thus, there were many criticisms of the position of the Lord Chancellor, not least being the lack of impartiality in dealing with appointments to the judiciary.

In June 2003, the Prime Minister announced an end to the role of the Lord Chancellor as a judge and as Speaker of the House of Lords. A Department of Constitutional Affairs was established which incorporates most of the responsibilities of the Lord Chancellor's Department. Lord Falconer was appointed as Secretary of State for Constitutional Affairs, with a seat in the Cabinet, and also became Speaker of the House of Lords. As part of the same package of reforms, the Government announced the establishment of an independent statutory Judicial Appointments Commission, and the creation of a new Supreme Court to replace the appellate jurisdiction of the House of Lords.

The Supreme Court of the United Kingdom

In recent years there have been mounting calls for the creation of a new independent Supreme Court, separating the highest appeal court from the House of Lords and removing the Law Lords from the legislature. On 12 June 2003 the Government announced its intention to do so and, in late 2004, the Constitutional Reform Act 2005 received Royal Assent.

The present Government believes that the new Supreme Court will reflect and enhance the independence of the judiciary from both the legislature and the executive. The decision to create the Supreme Court does not imply any dissatisfaction with the previous performance of the House of Lords as the UK's highest court of appeal; indeed, its judges have conducted themselves with the utmost integrity and independence throughout the years. However, the Government believes that the time has come to establish a new court, regulated by statute, as a body separate from Parliament. This will allow the UK to adhere more rigidly to the doctrine of the Separation of Powers.

The Supreme Court will be a United Kingdom body, legally separate from the Courts of England and Wales, which will take over the judicial functions of the Law Lords in the House of Lords and from the Judicial Committee of the Privy Council. The Supreme Court will be the final court of appeal in all matters under English law, Welsh law (to the extent that the Welsh Assembly make laws for Wales differing from those in England) and Northern Irish law. It will also be a court of record for appeals from the Court of Session in Scotland (there is no right of appeal beyond the High Court of Justiciary for criminal cases except in so far as devolution issues arise).

The Court will be located in a building separate from the Houses of Parliament and after a lengthy survey of suitable sites, including Somerset House, it has been decided that the location for the new court will be Middlesex Guildhall, in Parliament Square, Westminster, which is currently a Crown Court. The Court is expected to hold its first hearing in October 2009.

SOVEREIGNTY OF PARLIAMENT

This is also known as the legislative supremacy of Parliament and means that Acts of the UK Parliament are superior to any other source of law and that Parliament has unlimited law-making power. This peculiar concept marks the UK out from most other legislatures in the world.

The legal basis for the principle of parliamentary sovereignty

The traditional view is that of Dicey, which can be summarised in the following three tenets:

(a) no Act of the Queen in Parliament can be held invalid by a court of law;

(b) no Parliament can bind its successors as to the form or content of subsequent legislation; and

(c) there is no distinction in terms of procedure between ordinary statutes and those of constitutional importance.

The importance of Dicey's tenets has been reflected in a number of important decisions. In *Pickin* v *British Railways Board* (1974), Pickin sought to challenge the validity of an Act of Parliament, on the ground that Parliament had been misled during the course of the Bill through the legislature. The House of Lords held that no court of law can go behind an Act of Parliament, public or private, to investigate how it was introduced or what took place during its passage, even where irregularity or fraud was alleged.

In *Ellen Street Estates Ltd* v *Minister of Health* (1934), it was held that Parliament could not bind itself as to the form of subsequent legislation and could not properly enact that provisions in one statute could not be altered by a subsequent Act other than by express words. Maugham LJ stated:

> "The Legislature cannot, according to our constitution, bind itself as to the form of subsequent legislation, and it is impossible for Parliament to enact that in a subsequent statute dealing with the same subject-matter there can be no implied repeal. If in a subsequent Act, Parliament chooses to make it plain that the earlier statute is being to some extent repealed, effect must be given to that intention just because it is the will of the Legislature."

However, some matters authorised by legislation are of such a nature that they cannot be undone by a subsequent Act of Parliament. For example, s 4 of the Statute of Westminster 1931 states that no Act of Parliament passed after 1931 shall extend to a Dominion unless it is declared in the Act that the Dominion has requested and consented to it. This appears to acknowledge a territorial limit to the sovereignty of Parliament.

Practical limitations on parliamentary sovereignty

The possibility of disobedience

Though Parliament successfully enacted the poll tax legislation (the Abolition of Domestic Rates etc (Scotland) Act 1987 for Scotland and the Local Government Finance Act 1988 for England and Wales) the widespread disobedience and non-payment forced Parliament to repeal the legislation and introduce a more acceptable alternative. Dicey calls the possibility of disobedience an external limitation on the sovereignty of Parliament.

The beliefs and opinions of MPs

The Government will be unlikely to propose a piece of legislation which will not receive the support of Members of Parliament. Legislation cannot progress through the Parliament unless it has the support of a majority of MPs.

Consultation with interested parties

In consulting interest groups, the Government may bring about more acceptable legislation. For example, the British Veterinary Association was consulted in relation to the Dangerous Dogs Act 1991. Thus, consultation may inform and alter the content of appropriate legislation.

International agreements and world status

Since 1966, the UK has recognised the rights of the individual under the ECHR. The Convention has also been incorporated into the domestic law of the United Kingdom by virtue of the Human Rights Act 1998. Under the Human Rights Act, the House of Lords, the Judicial Committee of the Privy Council, the English High Court, the Court of Appeal, the Court of Session and the High Court of Justiciary (operating in an appeal capacity) have the ability to make declarations that an Act of the UK Parliament is incompatible with the provisions of the Convention. However, these declarations, though likely to be politically embarrassing, are non-binding.

Limitations arising from membership of the EU

As a result of its membership of the European Union, the UK has agreed to be bound by European law. The European Communities Act 1972 ensures the applicability of European law in the UK and states that all directly effective EU legislation creates an enforceable right within the UK and must be enforced by all courts and tribunals. It also states that all UK law must be applied subject to European law. Therefore, European law overarches our system of national law and, if there is any conflict, it is European law which prevails.

These provisions are fairly revolutionary in that they fundamentally undermine the concept of parliamentary sovereignty and the supremacy of the UK Parliament. The implications of the European Communities Act 1972 were discussed in great detail in the case of *R* v *Secretary of State for Transport, ex parte Factortame (No 2)* (1991). On appeal, it was affirmed by the House of Lords that an Act of Parliament contradicting EU legislation could not be enforced in the courts of the UK. Furthermore, since EU law had to be enforced, courts were entitled to issue orders to such effect. In effect, the 1972 Act allows European legislation to take precedence over that of the UK. There have been many positive effects of this principle, and some areas of UK law have been fundamentally changed for the better due to the influence of European law.

Recent debate on parliamentary sovereignty

The modern view is that the Diceyan concept of parliamentary sovereignty no longer exists in its original form. Dicey's theory attempts neatly to divide legal sovereignty from political sovereignty. But this cannot easily be achieved in today's climate of multi-layered constitutionalism, where the UK Government has devolved power to Scotland, Wales and Northern Ireland, while also creating a culture of citizens' rights via the Human Rights Act 1998. For example, under Diceyan sovereignty, the UK Government could abolish the Scottish Parliament or refuse to apply European legislation. However, because of political and diplomatic constraints, this would be difficult to achieve, though not impossible. The conflict between the traditional theory of sovereignty and the modern view is highlighted in the recent case of *Jackson* v *Attorney-General* (2005).

In the *Jackson* case, *obiter* comments made by Lords Steyn and Hope suggest that the concept of parliamentary sovereignty may be re-adjusted by the courts in the near future. Lord Hope, in particular, advocates that the Rule of Law enforced by the courts is the ultimate controlling factor upon which the UK constitution is based. Therefore, if Parliament were to attempt the unthinkable, such as the abolition of judicial review, then the courts would step in to protect citizens' rights under the Rule of Law.

On the other hand, further *obiter* comments made by Baroness Hale and Lord Bingham firmly support the continued existence of Diceyan sovereignty. Specifically, Baroness Hale expounds the view that although Parliament may be constrained in its exercise of power by international obligations and political realities, these constraints are purely political and diplomatic as opposed to legal and constitutional.

THE RULE OF LAW

The Rule of Law is a nebulous concept. It is not a legal doctrine as such but is more philosophical in form. The Rule of Law means that matters should be regulated by law, not by force, and in this form the principle is common to all civilised societies. In *X* v *Morgan Grampian Ltd* (1991), Lord Bridge said: "The maintenance of the rule of law is in every way as important in a free society as the democratic franchise. In our society the rule of law rests upon twin foundations: the sovereignty of the Queen in Parliament in making the law and the sovereignty of the Queen's courts in interpreting and applying the law."

The classic case on the rule of law is that of *Entick* v *Carrington* (1765), where the Home Secretary issued a general warrant which authorised

King's Messengers to break into Entick's house and seize private books and papers. Entick sued, claiming that the Home Secretary had acted unlawfully. The court decided that the warrant was illegal since there was no Act of Parliament or other law which authorised it. Thus, a Government Minister was held not to be above the law and the unlawful entry amounted to trespass.

In modern times the Rule of Law has become encapsulated in the following principles:

(a) *An absence of arbitrary power:* officials must be able to show legal authority for their actions, whether they be police constables or Ministers of the Crown.

(b) *Legal rights and duties must be determined, protected and enforced by the ordinary courts in accordance with the ordinary law.* Where rights are determined by bodies other than courts, such as tribunals, the proceedings of the decision-making body should be characterised by openness, fairness and impartiality.

(c) *The rights of individuals must yield to the rights of society as a whole only in accordance with specific rules of law recognised by the ordinary courts.* The emphasis is on the rights of the individual.

(d) *There must be clearly defined limits within which discretionary power is exercised.* There has been an increasing practice of conferring discretionary powers on Ministers by giving them authority to make delegated legislation. It is important that limits are set and adhered to.

(e) *There must be adequate safeguards for human rights.*

MINISTERIAL RESPONSIBILITY

The doctrine of ministerial responsibility performs the function of securing a level of accountability and control over the executive by Parliament. There are two aspects of responsibility: *collective* and *individual*. Under the doctrine of collective ministerial responsibility, all Ministers must either accept Cabinet decisions, or dissent publicly and resign, unless collective responsibility is waived by the Cabinet on a particular issue. This mechanism allows Governments to show a united front to Parliament and the public. Collective responsibility is followed slavishly by Governments since the executive must be seen as strong and there can be no doubt over its policies. Thus, if a Minister is placed under parliamentary pressure on a particular issue, the remainder of the Government will rally to give support since the policy will be a common one.

On the other hand, individual ministerial responsibility ensures that Ministers are responsible to Parliament for the administration of their individual departments, ie a Minister is accountable for not only personal decisions but also the actions and decisions of civil servants. The most infamous example of this doctrine can be found in the Crichel Down Affair, when the Air Ministry had compulsorily purchased land for defence purposes in 1938. By 1954, the land was no longer required and it was transferred to the Ministry of Agriculture which ultimately let it out to a tenant. The original owner of the land was neither consulted nor offered the opportunity to regain ownership. An inquiry into the affair discovered that many other landowners had been similarly affected and that the Ministry had acted in an underhand fashion. This resulted in widespread parliamentary and public condemnation and the Minister for Agriculture, Thomas Dugdale, resigned, taking full responsibility for the actions of his department. Similarly, in 1982, the Foreign Secretary, Lord Carrington, took personal responsibility for mismanagement of the Foreign and Commonwealth Office in failing to appreciate the threat of Argentine invasion of the Falklands.

In most cases, attempts are made to invoke ministerial responsibility by parliamentary questions or debate. In this way, parliamentary criticism can lead to public condemnation and might cause a resignation, but such resignations are becoming increasingly rare. In modern times, there has been a blurring of the distinction between questions of mismanagement and personal behaviour. Many resignations since 1945 have in fact involved questions of personal conduct, such as those of John Profumo in 1963 (who lied to the House) and David Mellor in 1992 (who was eventually forced out of the Cabinet following a war of attrition with the newspapers over his moral conduct). More recently, the former Home Secretary, David Blunkett, was forced to resign after factors in his private life led to the alleged speeding-up of an immigration application for the nanny of his son.

In recent years, given the growth in the number of executive Next Steps Agencies, the notion of ministerial responsibility has been identified with the idea of ministerial accountability, and a policy/operational dichotomy has developed in some government departments. Thus, the blame for many acts of mismanagement within a government department may be attached to the agency head or civil servant directorate involved instead of, or as well as, the Minister. Corrective action within the department will, however, be undertaken by the Minister.

Essential Facts

- The doctrine of the Separation of Powers recognises three separate organs of government, namely the legislature, the executive and the judiciary. Each organ should be vested with one main function of government only and should not interfere with the functions of another.

- It is debatable to what extent the Separation of Powers truly exists in the UK, since there are a number of areas of overlap. In particular, the office of Lord Chancellor has been a constant refutation of the doctrine; however, this has been altered by the Constitutional Reform Act 2005.

- Parliamentary sovereignty or the legislative supremacy of Parliament means that Acts of the UK Parliament are superior to any other source of law and that Parliament has unlimited law-making power.

- In modern times, parliamentary sovereignty has been somewhat eroded by a number of practical limitations, such as the UK's membership of the EU, and other international obligations.

- The Rule of Law is common to all civilised societies and represents an absence of arbitrary power. The Rule of Law recognises all citizens as being equal before the law and ensures that all state action is authorised by law.

- Countries which subscribe to the Rule of Law ought to have adequate safeguards in place to protect citizens from abuse of discretionary power and should also be able to protect fundamental human rights.

- Ministerial responsibility ensures that Ministers are responsible to Parliament for the administration of their individual departments, ie a Minister is accountable for not only personal decisions but also the actions and decisions of civil servants.

- In most cases, attempts are made to invoke ministerial responsibility by parliamentary questions or debate. In this way, parliamentary criticism can lead to public condemnation and may cause a resignation, but such resignations are becoming increasingly rare.

Essential Cases

Pickin v British Railways Board (1974): no court has the power to disregard an Act of Parliament or to question parliamentary procedure.

Ellen Street Estates Ltd v Minister of Health (1934): Parliament cannot bind itself as to the form of subsequent legislation nor properly enact that provisions in one statute cannot be altered by a subsequent Act other than by express words.

R v Secretary of State for Transport, ex parte Factortame (No 2) (1991): in effect confirms the practical limitations placed upon parliamentary sovereignty by EU membership. The European Communities Act 1972 allows European legislation to take precedence over that of the UK.

X v Morgan Grampian Ltd (1991): description of the Rule of Law.

Entick v Carrington (1765): classic exposition of the Rule of Law illustrating that power may not be exercised in an arbitrary fashion.

Jackson v Attorney-General (2005): discussion of the legality of passing a Bill utilising the Parliament Acts 1911 and 1949, ie without consent of the House of Lords. Notable for the discussion of the doctrine of parliamentary sovereignty in a multi-layered context.

4 THE JUDICIARY

It is a fundamental constitutional concept that the judiciary ought to be separate from the executive, ie the Government. This is one aspect of the Separation of Powers which is unequivocally accepted in the UK constitution, while all others are modified. The principles of the Rule of Law and equality before the law dictate that justice be administered impartially and universally, and this would be jeopardised if the courts were subject to the pressure of government. Thus, the independence of the judiciary is strictly preserved under the British constitution and, to this end, s 3 of the Constitutional Reform Act 2005 guarantees the independence of the judiciary in any part of the UK. Under this provision, Ministers must uphold the continued independence of the judiciary and must not seek to influence particular judicial decisions through any special access to the judiciary.

Although appointed in both Scotland and England by the executive, the judiciary is, by a combination of legal rules and extra-legal factors, clearly independent of both the executive and the legislature. The independence of the judiciary is widely recognised and, for that reason, the Government will occasionally entrust to members of the judiciary the task of conducting inquiries into events of political significance, for example Lord Hutton's inquiry into the circumstances surrounding the death of government scientist Dr David Kelly.

APPOINTMENT OF JUDGES IN SCOTLAND

Judicial appointments are a matter reserved to the executive. The two principal offices of the Lord President of the Court of Session and the Lord Justice-Clerk are appointed by the Queen on the advice of the Prime Minister, from a nomination of the First Minister (after consultation with the sitting Lord President and Lord Justice-Clerk unless, in either case, the office is vacant) (Scotland Act 1998, s 95(1) and (2)). Other judges of the Court of Session, sheriffs and sheriffs principal are appointed by the Queen on the recommendation of the First Minister (after consultation with the Lord President) (Scotland Act 1998, s 95(4)).

The appointment system has not been without its critics and, from the point of view of judicial independence, would be better served by an independent commission or board. The procedure would then be open, impartial and available to all. In an attempt to address this apparent lack of openness, the Scottish Executive published a Consultation Paper: *Judicial Appointments: An Inclusive Approach* (2000). In this document the Scottish Executive gave its commitment to changing the practice on judicial appointments. One of the main suggestions was that a Judicial Appointments Board be set up to handle the appointment of judges. The creation of such a body could allow the inclusion of lay people into the appointments process and would help to make the whole process more open.

Based upon this consultation paper, a number of proposals were announced in March 2001. The central elements of the proposals were:

- advertisements to be published for Court of Session Judges, sheriffs principal and sheriffs (both permanent and part-time);

- an independent Judicial Appointments Board, containing a balance of lay and legal members, chaired by a senior non-legal figure to be set up;

- the Board will advise the First Minister of its preferred candidate, together with a shortlist of other approved candidates in order of preference. The Board's proceedings will be confidential and only the names of successful candidates will be made public; and

- the First Minister will, as required by the Scotland Act 1998, consult the Lord President before making his recommendation to the Queen.

Based upon these proposals, the Judicial Appointments Board for Scotland was set up in March 2001 and began its work in June 2002 under the Chairmanship of Sir Neil McIntosh, CBE. As a result, the First Minister must now also consult and take advice from the Judicial Appointments Board for Scotland which has the remit of advertising judicial posts, interviewing potential candidates and providing a list of suitable candidates.

Eligibility

There are several statutory conditions of eligibility for judicial office. In order to become a sheriff or sheriff principal, a candidate must have been legally qualified as a solicitor or advocate for 10 years or more (Sheriff Courts (Scotland) Act 1971, s 5). Historically, candidates appointed to the High Court or the Court of Session would normally have been advocates but, since 1990, a new regime has widened the categories of those eligible candidates and provides that sheriffs principal, and sheriffs who have held office for not less than 5 years, are eligible (Law Reform (Miscellaneous

Provisions) (Scotland) Act 1990, s 35(1)). Likewise, solicitors enjoying extended rights of audience in the Court of Session or the High Court for a similar period may be appointed.

Rules concerning the removal of judges

Under common law, judges hold office *ad vitam aut culpam* – for life and during good behaviour. This rule has arisen partly from custom, and also from the Claim of Right 1689. The Judicial Pensions and Retirement Act 1993 has introduced a new retirement age for Court of Session judges and sheriffs of 70, with the possibility of an extension to 75.

When it becomes necessary to remove a judge, there are differences in procedure in Scotland and England. In England, the process has been statutory since at least 1701, and the current legislation can be found in the Supreme Court Act 1981. Normally, judges in the supreme courts are removable by the Queen, on receipt of an address presented to her by both Houses of Parliament. But the provisions of the 1981 Act do not extend to Scotland. Thus, up until the enactment of the Scotland Act 1998, there was no statutory mechanism for the removal of a Court of Session judge. Now, s 95 of the 1998 Act lays down a procedure for the removal of a Court of Session judge. A judge may be removed from office by the Queen on the recommendation of the First Minister. The First Minister may make such a recommendation only if the Parliament, on a motion made by the First Minister, resolves that it should be made. The First Minister may seek such a resolution only if he has received a written report from a tribunal constituted under s 95, concluding that the judge is unfit for office by reason of inability, neglect of duty or misbehaviour. Furthermore, if the report relates to either the Lord President or the Lord Justice-Clerk, then the First Minister must consult the Prime Minister before making a recommendation.

In the case of sheriffs, a statutory procedure has existed for some years. It is set out in the Sheriff Courts (Scotland) Act 1971, and empowers the Scottish Ministers, on receiving a report from the Lord President and the Lord Justice-Clerk, to suspend or remove any sheriff from office, on clearly defined grounds of inability, neglect of duty or misbehaviour. If removal is contemplated, then the order is laid before both Houses of Parliament. These provisions were invoked in 1975, when the political activities of Sheriff Peter Thomson, who was involved in the Scottish Plebiscite Society, were deemed unacceptable, and he was removed from office. A more recent example can be seen in the case of *Stewart* v *Secretary of State for Scotland* (1998), where Sheriff Ewen Stewart sought judicial review of the Secretary of State's order removing him from office. His attempt to challenge the removal procedures was unsuccessful.

TEMPORARY JUDGES

In recent years, the Government has been enthusiastic about the idea of using more temporary judges. In Scotland, there have been important developments, particularly concerning temporary sheriffs. In the case of *Starrs* v *Ruxton* (2000) an issue arose as to the compatibility of a temporary sheriff's status with an accused person's right to a fair hearing before an independent and impartial tribunal (Art 6 of the European Convention on Human Rights). The High Court held that possible hopes of appointment to a permanent position, as well as the short-term nature of the office, compromised the independence of the temporary sheriff and that the most important factor was the absence of security of tenure. Accordingly, Lord Cullen stated that it was necessary that such a situation be remedied and that legal guarantees of the independence of the judiciary be put in place.

In response, the Bail, Judicial Appointments etc (Scotland) Act 2000 was passed by the Scottish Parliament. Sections 6 and 7 of the 2000 Act deal with the abolition of temporary sheriffs in Scotland and create the new office of part-time sheriff. Whether part-time appointments completely conform with Art 6 of the European Convention on Human Rights is a further moot point. They do, however, provide security of tenure for a fixed term and so guarantee a greater freedom from interference by the executive.

JUDICIAL PRIVILEGE

Judges enjoy an absolute privilege in relation to actions of damages in delict. There is no right of action against the higher judiciary in what they do or say in their judicial capacity. The Crown Proceedings Act 1947 allows injured parties the right to sue the Crown, and to seek a remedy or damages on the basis of vicarious liability for the actions of Crown Servants. But s 2 of the 1947 Act clearly states that the Crown is not vicariously liable for acts or omissions of a member of the judiciary. Thus, judges continue to enjoy immunity at common law in actions of delict.

Judges also enjoy protection under the criminal law. At common law, it is a crime to slander a judge or magistrate in reference to his official conduct or capacity. Threatening a judge is also a crime, as is bribing a judge, or attempting to do so.

IMPARTIALITY OF JUDGES

Judges are expected to abstain from political activities, and matters of public controversy generally. In 1955, the Lord Chancellor, Lord Kilmuir, laid down rules which sought to prevent judges from making appearances in any medium without first consulting the Lord Chancellor. Kilmuir felt that this would allow judges to isolate themselves from the media and any controversies. The influence of the Kilmuir rules have been somewhat eroded today, in that the passage of time has seen judges publish memoirs, write articles, appear on broadcasts and generally let their opinions be known. In 1987, this led to Lord Mackay removing the need to seek permission from the Lord Chancellor and since then judges have become increasingly vocal on controversial subjects.

The political neutrality of the judiciary is ensured by their exclusion from the House of Commons, the Scottish Parliament and the National Assembly for Wales, by virtue of statute. It was historically true that Scottish judges sat in the House of Commons until excluded by statute in 1733 by s 4 of the Parliamentary Elections (Scotland) Act 1733. This came about because the then Prime Minister, Robert Walpole, faced a looming General Election, and the determined opposition of the Lord Justice-Clerk, who sought to enter Parliament against Walpole. A Bill on the Scottish electoral process came before Parliament which sought, among other things, to prevent judges of the Court of Session from standing for election. The plan backfired, however, as the Lord Justice-Clerk resigned from the Bench, returned to the Bar, and was elected MP for Clackmannanshire.

Judicial salaries are charged on the Consolidated Fund. This means that there is no need to seek annual authority from Parliament, and no opportunity to debate the matter. The Review Body on Senior Salaries provides independent advice to the Prime Minister, the Lord Chancellor and the Secretary of State for Defence on the remuneration of holders of judicial office. The Government usually accepts the recommendations of this body.

The House of Commons will not discuss the conduct of a judge, except on a substantive motion (a motion specifically criticising a named judge, or supporting an address for his removal from office). It would appear that the Scottish Parliament will more readily discuss the conduct of a judge. For example, as a result of the case of *HM Advocate* v *Watt* (2002), the Scottish Parliament criticised Lord Abernethy for his comments upon a case where a man had been charged with rape and his decision that the accused had no case to answer where there was no evidence that he had used some degree of force or violent threats.

The competence of a judge cannot be impugned at Ministerial Question Time or some equivalent occasion, for the substantive motion is the appropriate parliamentary mechanism for subjecting a judge to scrutiny and debate. Recently, a motion was moved for the removal of Lord Lane, after the "Birmingham Six" appeal, but this motion failed.

Absence of bias

Judges must be impartial between the parties before them if true administration of justice is to be achieved. Litigants must have confidence in the impartiality of judges hearing a particular controversy or dispute. In this respect, the common law rules of natural justice protect against bias. This is enshrined specifically in the rule against bias – *nemo iudex in causa sua*. Under this concept, the exercise of jurisdiction may be excluded on the ground of relationship to one of the parties, or of interest in the matters involved in the case. Where the matter is one of interest, the rule is that *any pecuniary* interest will disqualify – for example, if a judge were a shareholder in a company which was one of the parties to an action, he would be disqualified (*Grand National Canal Co v Dimes* (1852)). Where the interest is *non-pecuniary*, it must be shown to be *substantial* before disqualification can be made (*Wildridge v Anderson* (1897)).

Essential Facts

- The independence of the judiciary is a fundamental principle of the UK constitution. Judges must be free from the pressure of government in order to achieve fairness and impartiality. To this end, their security of tenure is protected by a number of legal rules and Acts of Parliament.
- Judicial appointments are a matter reserved to the executive. The Lord President of the Court of Session and the Lord Justice-Clerk are appointed by the Queen on the advice of the Prime Minister, from a nomination of the First Minister (after consultation with the sitting Lord President and Lord Justice-Clerk unless, in either case, the office is vacant) (Scotland Act 1998, s 95(1) and (2)).
- Other judges of the Court of Session, sheriffs and sheriffs principal are appointed by the Queen on the recommendation of the First Minister (after consultation with the Lord President) (Scotland Act 1998, s 95(4)).

- The Judicial Appointments Board for Scotland has the remit of advertising judicial posts, interviewing potential candidates and providing a list of suitable candidates. The First Minister must consult and take advice from the Judicial Appointments Board for Scotland during the appointments process.
- In order to become a sheriff or sheriff principal, a candidate must have been legally qualified as a solicitor or advocate for 10 years or more (Sheriff Courts (Scotland) Act 1971, s 5).
- Candidates seeking appointment to the High Court or Court of Session would normally have been advocates but, since 1990, a new regime has widened the categories of those eligible candidates and provides that sheriffs principal, and sheriffs who have held office for not less than 5 years, are eligible (Law Reform (Miscellaneous Provisions) (Scotland) Act 1990, s 35(1)). Likewise, solicitors enjoying extended rights of audience in the Court of Session or High Court for a similar period may be appointed.

Essential Cases

Stewart v Secretary of State for Scotland (1998): Sheriff Ewen Stewart sought judicial review of the Secretary of State's order removing him from office. His attempt to challenge the removal procedures was unsuccessful.

Starrs v Ruxton (2000): an issue arose as to the compatibility of a temporary sheriff's status with an accused person's right to a fair hearing before an independent and impartial tribunal (Art 6 of the European Convention on Human Rights). The High Court held that possible hopes of appointment to a permanent position, as well as the short-term nature of the office, compromised the independence of the temporary sheriff and that the most important factor was the absence of security of tenure. Accordingly, temporary sheriffs were abolished by virtue of the Bail, Judicial Appointments etc (Scotland) Act 2000.

5 THE MONARCHY

The monarchy is the oldest institution of government in the United Kingdom and, although absolute power has been progressively reduced over the centuries, the monarch retains a significant constitutional role as Head of State. The United Kingdom is a constitutional monarchy – that is to say, it has a monarchical government established under a system which acknowledges a hereditary monarch as Head of State. The Queen is officially recognised as such and plays a formal role in the work of Parliament, but her position can be seen as more ceremonial in form rather than executive. Practically speaking, the Prime Minister, whose power is derived directly or indirectly from democratic elections, is the head of government and the actions of government are carried out on behalf of the monarch.

The history of the monarchy, however, is very much alive in the numerous palaces and residences still in existence across the UK, and many royal traditions continue to be celebrated. Walter Bagehot, in his classic study *The English Constitution*, referred to the "dignified capacity" of the Sovereign and many commentators are of the opinion that the continuity and stability provided by the Sovereign is fundamentally important for the stability of the British constitution. The purpose of this chapter is to examine the legislation and other legal rules which govern the position of the monarch today and make the current Queen very much an important part of the constitution.

TITLE TO THE CROWN AND SUCCESSION

Title is derived from the Act of Settlement 1700, which was subsequently extended to Scotland by Art II of the Act of Union 1707. Under the Act of Settlement, succession to the throne is settled upon "the heirs of the body (being Protestant) of Princess Sophia", the Electress of Hanover and grand-daughter of James I. The title descends lineally, according to feudal rules, with the rule of male primogeniture applying, ie males being preferred to females despite the fact that an elder female may be chronologically next in line to the throne. Any member of the Royal Family succeeding to the throne must:

(a) take the coronation oath, by virtue of the Coronation Oath Act 1688;

(b) declare himself to be a faithful Protestant, by virtue of the Bill of Rights 1688 and the Act of Settlement 1700;

(c) swear to maintain the Church of Scotland and the Church of England, by virtue of the Act of Union 1707;

(d) enter into communion with the Church of England, by virtue of the Act of Settlement 1700; and

(e) not be (or marry) a Roman Catholic, by virtue of the Bill of Rights 1688 and the Act of Union 1707.

Title to the Crown is a parliamentary one, and the succession may be altered only by Parliament. This has happened only one since 1714, when His Majesty's Declaration of Abdication Act 1936, provided that Edward VIII's abdication should take effect since he wanted to marry divorcée Wallis Simpson. The 1936 Act further provided that the brother next in line, George VI, should succeed to the throne and that Edward VIII's issue and their descendants should have no right of succession.

The title

The present title is regulated under the Royal Titles Act 1953 which emerged as a result of an agreement by Commonwealth Ministers. The 1953 Act authorised the adoption by the Queen, for use in relation to the UK and those territories for which the UK Government is responsible for their foreign relations, of such style or titles as Her Majesty may think fit. By 1953 the Commonwealth included a republic – India – of which Elizabeth could not be Queen. So the present Queen Elizabeth is known as:

> "Elizabeth II by the Grace of God of the United Kingdom of Great Britain and Northern Ireland and of Her other Realms and Territories Queen, Head of the Commonwealth, Defender of the Faith."

In *MacCormick* v *Lord Advocate* (1953), the use of the title "ER II", signifying "Queen Elizabeth II", was challenged in Scotland as a contravention of the Treaty of Union, since there had never been a "Queen Elizabeth I" of Scotland. The Court of Session held that the numeral did not derive from the Royal Titles Act 1953 but from the proclamation at the Queen's accession in 1952; that nothing in the Treaty of Union prohibited the adoption of the style; and that, in any case, MacCormick had neither title nor interest to sue.

Minority, incapacity, illness and temporary absence

Such events are covered by the Regency Acts 1937, 1943 and 1953. These Acts provide for a regent who may exercise the functions of the monarch should they be physically or mentally incapacitated, absent or in minority (under the age of 18). Prior to 1937, Regency Acts were passed only when necessary. However, the Regency Act 1937 provided specific scope for a regent in law and also established the post of Counsellor in State to act on the monarch's behalf when temporarily absent. The present Counsellors of State are the Duke of Edinburgh and the four adults next in succession (provided they have reached the age of 21): currently the Prince of Wales, the Duke of York, the Earl of Wessex and Prince William.

The regent is normally the person next in line to the throne, not excluded by the Act of Settlement 1700, and a British subject, of full age, domiciled in the UK. Regency is automatic on the succession of a minor; in the case of incapacity, a declaration has to be made by any three of the following: the monarch's spouse, the Lord Chancellor, the Speaker, the Lord Chief Justice and the Master of the Rolls. The declaration is made to the Privy Council and communicated to the Commonwealth. The regent may exercise all royal functions except assenting to a Bill to change the order of succession or to alter the Act of Security of the Church of Scotland 1706.

Currently, under the provisions of the Regency Act 1937, Prince Charles, Prince of Wales, would act as regent in the event of the incapacity of the Queen. The next four individuals in the line of succession would be eligible to succeed or be regents in their own right. The first minor is Princess Eugenie of York. If she were to succeed while under the age of 18, her uncle, Prince Edward, Earl of Wessex would be regent under the 1937 Act. Ultimately, Parliament decides the regent, and may choose to pass a new Regency Act, in this case to make Prince Philip, Duke of Edinburgh, or Princess Anne, Princess Royal, regent in place of Edward.

FINANCING THE MONARCHY

The monarchy is often described as an expensive institution, with royal finances clouded by secrecy. In reality, the Royal Household is committed to ensuring that public money is spent efficiently, and to making royal finances open and transparent. The Royal Household publishes an annual summary of Head of State expenditure, accompanied by a full report on all royal public finances (these reports can be accessed through the monarch's official website at www.royal.gov.uk).

Sources of funding

There are four distinct sources of funding for the monarchy, or officials of the Royal Household acting on the monarch's behalf, in both public and private capacities. These are:

(i)   the Civil List;
(ii) Grants-in-Aid for the Upkeep of Royal Palaces and Royal Travel;
(iii) the Privy Purse; and
(iv) the Queen's personal income.

The Civil List

This is the sum of money provided to the Queen from Parliament by virtue of the Civil List Acts 1952, 1972 and 1975. It is often misunderstood as a "salary" for the Queen but this is not the case. Rather, it is a source of funding for the Queen's official work as Head of State and Head of the Commonwealth, and meets the expenses of the Queen's Household. The Civil List has been in existence since the Restoration of the monarchy in 1660 but was reformed in 1760 by George III. Since then, the whole cost of civil government has been met by Parliament, in return for the surrender of the hereditary revenues of the Crown including the income from Crown Estates. The Estates are administered by Crown Estates Commissioners under the terms of the Crown Estate Act 1961. During the year 2005–06, the amount of hereditary revenue paid to the Treasury from the Crown Estate was £190.8 million. This is an excellent arrangement for the Government when one considers that, in the same year, Civil List expenditure amounted to only £11.2 million.

Grants-in-Aid

Occupied royal palaces in England are held by the Queen as Sovereign and are used to fulfil her role as Head of State. An annual vote is taken by Parliament to cover the cost of the upkeep of the royal residences for both official and public use. In the year 2005–06, the Grant-in-Aid approved by Parliament was £14.3 million. This sum is administered by the Department for Culture, Media and Sport but, since 1991, the Property section of the Royal Household has held daily management and operational responsibilities. The costs of maintaining the Palace of Holyroodhouse are met directly by the Scotland Office and administered by Historic Scotland. The unoccupied palaces receive no government funding and their upkeep is provided for through visitor admissions and other related sources of income.

The Royal Household also receives an annual Royal Travel Grant-in-Aid from Parliament, through the Department for Transport (DfT). The administration of this grant is supervised by the DfT and the Royal Household must submit detailed quarterly and annual reports which contain budget information and a rolling 5-year plan. Most of the royal travel budget is spent on the Queen's helicopter and chartered aircraft used for overseas visits. Official car travel for the Queen is paid for from the Civil List and for other members of the Royal Family from private sources. The Royal Travel Grant-in-Aid for the year 2005–06 was £5.9 million.

The Privy Purse

This refers to the income obtained from the Duchy of Lancaster which is used to meet both official and private expenditure incurred by the Queen. Since 1399, the Duchy of Lancaster has remained separate from the Crown Estate and consists of a portfolio of land, property and assets held in trust for the Sovereign in his role as the Duke of Lancaster. The main function of the Duchy is to provide an independent source of income for the Queen. It is currently used to meet any expenditure not covered by the Civil List and also to pay for the expenses of other members of the Royal Family. The net revenues paid to the Sovereign during 2005–06 were in the region of £8 million.

The Queen's personal income

Used to meet purely private expenditure, this source of income is derived from the Queen's private estates and investments. The public are often mistaken in thinking that these include the royal palaces, the Crown Jewels and other treasures. But such things are in fact held by Her Majesty as Sovereign, and must pass on to her successor. The Queen does, however, own, as a private individual, the estates of Balmoral and Sandringham. No accurate measure of the Queen's private income can be made but it is thought to be somewhere in the region of £1.15 billion or more.

The Prince of Wales

The Prince of Wales does not receive any funding from the Civil List. Both his private and work lives are overwhelmingly provided for by the Duchy of Cornwall. The Duchy was created in 1337 by Edward II for his heir and its primary function is to provide an income for the current and future Princes of Wales. The Duchy consists of approximately 54,000 hectares of predominantly agricultural land and, in the year 2005–06, provided the Prince with an income of just over £14 million.

Additional members of the Royal Family

Only the Queen and the Duke of Edinburgh receive annual parliamentary allowances. All other allowances are now repaid by the Queen from her personal income. Thus, for example, HRH The Princess Royal receives £228,000 in the form of a parliamentary allowance – but this is paid back directly to the Treasury by the Queen.

Taxation

Since 1992, the Queen has voluntarily agreed to be subject to the same taxes as ordinary citizens. This includes income tax, council tax, value added tax and capital gains tax. However, there are a few areas where the Queen is exempt from normal taxation. This occurs most notably in relation to inheritance tax, since bequests from Sovereign to Sovereign are exempt. This is necessary in order to maintain impartiality and financial independence.

The Duchy of Cornwall is exempt from taxation but the Prince of Wales pays voluntary contributions to the Exchequer. All other members of the Royal Family are subject to taxation in the same way as ordinary citizens.

DUTIES OF THE SOVEREIGN

The duties of the Sovereign are wide and varied. As Head of State, the Queen must undertake certain constitutional duties and many formal acts of government require her participation. These include signing state documents, receiving reports from ambassadors, reading Cabinet papers, giving audiences to the Prime Minister and visiting Commonwealth Ministers. The Queen also attends many state occasions, such as the State Opening of Parliament each session. In her role as Head of State, she must be politically neutral, but retains the rights to be consulted, to encourage and to warn. What influence the Sovereign will actually have on her Ministers will depend on a number of factors, including the experience and the character of the individuals and the policy area concerned.

As "Head of Nation", the Queen has a less formal role but one which is more important in terms of social and cultural functions. These include acting as a figurehead for national identity and unity, carrying out charitable work, visiting local communities and recognising achievement through honours, awards and financial support.

When both roles are combined, it is recognised that the monarch provides a large measure of stability within the UK constitution. Political and economic trends may fluctuate wildly, but the system of constitutional monarchy provides a stable foundation for the country. The Queen has an unrivalled knowledge of politics within the UK and successive Prime Ministers have been able to benefit from her insights through weekly audiences.

THE ROYAL PREROGATIVE

The Royal Prerogative is difficult to define. It has been described as those inherent legal attributes which are unique to the Crown. Inherent in that they are derived from custom and the common law, rather than statute; legal in that they are recognised and enforced by the UK courts. Furthermore, the courts may also determine their limits, as in *The Case of Proclamations* (1611) in which a proclamation by the King, forbidding building construction in and around London, was held to be unlawful by the courts.

According to Dicey, the Royal Prerogative was "the residue of discretionary or arbitrary authority which at any given time is legally left in the hands of the Crown". The use of the word "residue" in Dicey's definition is important, since the prerogative powers cannot be enlarged. They exist merely in the form of residual powers. Prerogatives have been abolished or diminished by statute (such as the Crown Proceedings Act 1947) and more and more of the prerogative powers have been transferred to the Government. There are, however, still some which remain "personal" to the Sovereign.

The personal prerogatives of the monarch

The main personal prerogatives of the monarch are often listed as follows:

- the appointment of a Prime Minister;
- the dissolution of Parliament;
- the dismissal of Ministers;
- giving the Royal Assent; and
- conferring various appointments and honours.

However, the extent to which the Queen exercises her own discretion in these matters is a topic of great debate.

The appointment of a Prime Minister

The Queen's choice of Prime Minister is governed by convention and political realities. She must appoint the person who can form a Government which will have the confidence of the House of Commons. Normally, this will be the leader of the party which has a majority of seats in the House. But a change of Prime Minister may occasionally become necessary through resignation, death or dismissal. Dismissal is very unusual and, indeed, has never occurred since the end of Queen Victoria's reign. Resignation, however, is more common and may occur in a number of circumstances:

(a) through defeat in a General Election;

(b) through internal dissension causing the collapse of a Government;

(c) as a result of a defeat on a vote of no confidence in the House of Commons;

(d) due to ill health, old age or other personal reasons; and

(e) through the governing party persuading the Prime Minister to leave office, since he has become a political liability.

In such circumstances, the monarch will normally choose the leader of the party which wins a majority in an election. But if no party wins an overall majority, as in February 1974, it may not be immediately clear whether the existing Prime Minister or the Leader of the Opposition or some other party leader will have sufficient support to govern effectively. In February 1974 the Conservative holding was reduced from 323 seats to 296, while the Labour Party had 301 seats but no overall majority in the House of Commons of (then) 635. The Prime Minister, Edward Heath, did not resign but instead tried to form a coalition with the 14 Liberal MPs. Having failed to do so, he resigned and the Queen sent for Harold Wilson, as leader of the largest party in the House of Commons, and he formed a minority Government and thus became Prime Minister. Consequently, in such difficult situations, the Queen's position can be summarised as follows:

(a) give the existing Prime Minister (if there is one) or the leader of the largest party an opportunity to form a coalition or reach an agreement about forming a Government;

(b) if that fails, send for the leader of the other party and give him a similar opportunity;

(c) in the unlikely event of that failing, the existing Prime Minister would presumably ask for a dissolution and a fresh General Election.

This is all very straightforward under a two-party system but if multi-party politics should become the norm in Britain, perhaps arising from the introduction of proportional representation for elections at Westminster, the conventions of the two-party system would be of limited guidance to the monarch. The question would inevitably have to be solved by inter-party bargaining. But if this failed, it could fall to the monarch to exercise a personal judgement. This would be highly controversial, and would have major political repercussions. The question to be answered in such a hypothetical situation is: should the decision be left to the Queen and her personal advisers or should the decision be taken by, for example, the Speaker of the House of Commons, or a ballot of all MPs? The answer is a moot point.

Dissolution of Parliament

In the absence of statutorily fixed-term Parliaments, the Queen may dissolve Parliament and cause a General Election to be held. Usually, she acts on the advice of the Prime Minister and, since 1918, no Cabinet decision has been necessary. The question to be asked is: are there any circumstances in which the Queen can refuse a dissolution requested by the Prime Minister? There is no modern example of a categorical refusal within the UK. But it is thought that the Queen would be justified in refusing a dissolution request to a Prime Minister who has lost the confidence of his party and who sees a dissolution as a means of escape or salvation.

It is also possible that the Queen may be entitled to refuse a dissolution if a General Election had been held only a short time previously. This question was canvassed after the election of February 1974. The minority Labour Government was faced with the possibility of immediate defeat in the House of Commons in a division on the Address in reply to the Queen's Speech. The Prime Minister publicly declared his intention to seek an immediate dissolution. As it happened, the challenge to the Government did not materialise and the Queen granted Prime Minister Wilson's later request for a dissolution in September 1974, for an October election.

Again, as with the power to appoint a Prime Minister, an era of multi-party governmental groupings and coalition Governments might lead to the monarch having to exercise personal (and political) judgement.

The dismissal of Ministers

The Queen has a prerogative power to dismiss Ministers either singly or collectively. In reality, the fate of individual Ministers lies with the Prime Minister and no-one, for example, would have expected the Queen to ask former Home Secretary David Blunkett to resign following his political misdemeanours. As for Governments, none in the UK has been unequivocally dismissed since 1783. So, in modern times, it would certainly be viewed as unconstitutional for the monarch to dismiss a Government except in the most extraordinary circumstances. But the monarch's power is said to survive in case a Government should attempt to destroy the democratic or parliamentary bases of the British constitution. Thus, if a Government attempted to prolong the life of Parliament in order to avoid defeat at a General Election, it is thought that the monarch would be justified in dismissing the Government. The position would be the same if a Government insisted on remaining in office after having lost a vote of confidence in the House of Commons.

The Royal Assent

Royal Assent is the final stage necessary in order for a Bill to become a formal Act of Parliament and pass into law. The Queen has, in strict legal terms, the power to refuse to give Royal Assent to a Bill. However, in modern times it has become a convention that the monarch is bound to give assent to any Bill, except in extraordinary circumstances. The last time assent was given by the Crown in person was in 1854 and assent has not been refused since 1707, when Queen Anne refused to consent to the Scottish Militia Bill.

Conferring appointments and honours

Although the majority of Crown appointments and honours are made by the Queen on the advice of the Prime Minister, some remain within her personal gift. The Queen appoints members of her own Household. Appointments to the Orders of the Garter and of the Thistle, the Order of Merit and the Royal Victorian Order are also within her personal discretion.

The executive prerogatives

Although most of government today depends on powers granted by Acts of Parliament, there are still some residual areas where the Crown, as Her Majesty's Government, derives its authority from common law, rather than statute. Ministers are responsible to Parliament for the exercise of prerogative powers, and may, with certain exceptions, be questioned about their exercise.

The extent of the prerogative today

The prerogative covers various areas and in some, where an antiquated power has not been used in modern times, the law is uncertain. But the main areas where prerogative powers are used in relation to today are:

(a) the legislature, eg to summon, prorogue and dissolve Parliament, to create peers, and to legislate by Order in Council;

(b) the judicial system, eg to appoint judges and magistrates and to grant leave to appeal to the Judicial Committee of the Privy Council;

(c) foreign affairs;

(d) the armed forces;

(e) appointments and honours;

(f) various privileges and immunities;

(g) powers in defence of the realm; and

(h) miscellaneous prerogatives, including the right to sturgeon, certain whales and swans, to treasure trove, and to mine precious metals.

The effect of statute on prerogative powers

Parliament can, by express words, abolish or restrict the prerogative and may link this to a grant of statutory powers covering the same area. But sometimes Parliament creates a statutory scheme without expressly abolishing prerogative rights in the same area. In such a situation the Crown must abide by statutory restrictions on its power and cannot fall back on its original absolute prerogative. The leading authority on this is *Attorney-General* v *De Keyser's Royal Hotel* (1920), where the Government took possession of a hotel in London in order to house army officers. Afterwards, the hotel owners sued the Crown for compensation, relying upon the Defence Act 1842. The Government argued that the hotel had been occupied under the prerogative power to take property for the defence of the realm, which imported no duty to pay compensation. The House of Lords held that the Government could not lawfully act on the prerogative power when there was a statute which authorised it to take the property and provided for compensation.

Essential Facts

- The Government of the UK consists of the monarch, the Prime Minister, the Cabinet and other Ministers of the Crown.
- The UK has a constitutional monarchy: that is to say it has a monarchical Government established under a system which acknowledges a hereditary monarch as Head of State.
- The Queen is officially recognised as Head of State and plays a formal role in the work of Parliament, but her position can be seen as more ceremonial in form rather than executive.
- Title to the throne is governed by the Act of Settlement 1700. The monarch must be a Protestant; Roman Catholics and those married to Roman Catholics are disqualified. Succession is also governed by the rule of male primogeniture.
- There are four distinct sources of funding for the monarchy: the Civil List; Grants-in-Aid for the Upkeep of Royal Palaces and Royal Travel; the Privy Purse; and the monarch's personal income. Only the Queen and the Duke of Edinburgh receive annual parliamentary allowances. All other allowances are now repaid by the Queen from her personal income.
- The duties of the monarch are varied and differ depending on whether she is acting in her capacity as Head of State or Head of Nation.
- As Head of State, the Queen must undertake certain constitutional duties and many formal acts of government require her participation. Her role as Head of Nation is a less formal role but one which is more important in terms of social and cultural functions, including acting as a figurehead for national identity and unity, and carrying out charitable work.
- The Royal Prerogative is derived from the residual common law powers of the monarch and dates back to an era when the monarch could do whatever he wished. It has been described by Dicey as "the residue of discretionary power which at any given time is legally left in the hands of the Crown".
- Today, however, the prerogative powers are normally exercised by Government Ministers in the name of the Queen. Such powers include declaring war, making treaties and pardoning criminals, although the Queen still exercises some prerogative powers including choosing a Prime Minister and dissolving Parliament.

Essential Cases

MacCormick v Lord Advocate (1953): the use of the title "ER II", signifying "Queen Elizabeth II", was challenged in Scotland as a contravention of the Treaty of Union, since there had never been a "Queen Elizabeth I" of Scotland. The Court of Session held that the numeral did not derive from the Royal Titles Act 1953 but from the proclamation at the Queen's accession in 1952; that nothing in the Treaty of Union prohibited the adoption of the style; and that in any case MacCormick had neither title nor interest to sue.

The Case of Proclamations (1611): limits of the exercise of the Royal Prerogative, subject to control by the courts. The King forbidding building construction in and around London, subject to penalty, was held to be unlawful by the courts.

Attorney-General v De Keyser's Royal Hotel (1920): concerned the effect of statute on prerogative powers. The Government took possession of a hotel in London, in order to house army officers. Afterwards, the hotel owners sued the Crown for compensation, relying upon the Defence Act 1842. The Government argued that the hotel had been occupied under the prerogative power to take property for the defence of the realm, which imported no duty to pay compensation. The House of Lords held that the Government could not lawfully act on the prerogative power when there was a statute which authorised it to take the property and provided for compensation.

6 THE UNITED KINGDOM PARLIAMENT

The Parliament of the United Kingdom consists of three distinct elements:

- the monarch;
- the House of Commons (an elected body); and
- the House of Lords (an unelected body).

THE MONARCH

In Chapter 5, we have already examined the important role played by the monarch in relation to Parliament. By convention, the Queen must give Royal Assent to Bills which have been passed by the House of Commons and the House of Lords to enable them to become Acts of the Queen in Parliament. The Queen also summons Parliament after each General Election and dissolves it at the end of its term.

THE HOUSE OF COMMONS

The House of Commons currently consists of 646 men and women known as Members of Parliament or MPs. They are elected during General Elections which are held every 4 or 5 years, reflecting the maximum life of a Parliament. They are chosen by virtue of a method known as the relative majority, or "first past the post" system, whereby a candidate who receives the most votes in a parliamentary constituency will be elected to Parliament. There are many criticisms of this method of election, chiefly that it leads to a Parliament which does not necessarily reflect the political choices of the majority of voters who choose losing candidates. Even if the runner-up candidate in a constituency has lost by a handful of votes, he does not receive any right to sit in Parliament. Consequently, a number of calls have been made to replace the current system with one which is more proportionate. There are a number of alternatives, including the Additional Member System (AMS), used by the Scottish Parliament, which seeks to achieve a closer link between the number of votes cast for each candidate and the number of seats won.

The right to vote

Citizens entitled to vote must be UK residents aged 18 or over who are:

- British citizens;
- Commonwealth citizens;
- citizens of the Irish Republic; and
- registered in the register of parliamentary elections.

The following groups of people are not allowed to vote in elections to the UK Parliament, either under pre-existing law or under the Representation of the People Act 1983 (as amended):

- aliens (people who are not British, Commonwealth or Irish citizens);
- minors (those aged under 18);
- members of the House of Lords;
- offenders detained in a mental hospital;
- convicted prisoners while detained in a penal institution or unlawfully at large having escaped from confinement;
- undischarged bankrupts; and
- persons guilty of specific electoral offences.

Disqualification from membership

The Parliamentary Elections Act 1695 states that no person under the age of 21 shall be eligible for election to Parliament. There are a number of other important disqualifications, most of which are embodied in statute (see, generally, the House of Commons Disqualification Act 1975):

- aliens;
- persons suffering from mental illness;
- members of the House of Lords;
- undischarged bankrupts;
- persons guilty of particular electoral offences;
- persons sentenced to a term of imprisonment exceeding 1 year;
- persons guilty of treason;
- members of foreign legislatures outside the Commonwealth (excluding the European Parliament and Ireland); and
- holders of certain public offices, such as judges or police officers.

Previously, clergy who had been Episcopally ordained, ie by a bishop, were disqualified from membership. This applied to clergy of the Church of England and Church of Ireland, and ministers of the Church of Scotland, under the terms of s 1 of the House of Commons (Clergy

Disqualification) Act 1801; and to Roman Catholic priests through s 9 of the Roman Catholic Relief Act 1829. However, the House of Commons (Removal of Clergy Disqualifications) Act 2001 has now altered the law in this area. Under s 1, a person is not disqualified from being or being elected as a member of the House of Commons merely because he has been ordained or is a minister of any religious denomination. All of the pre-existing legislation has been repealed.

Functions

Representative

A very important part of an MP's job is representing his constituents and taking up issues on their behalf. Most MPs hold surgeries in their constituencies to enable them to keep in touch with the people who elected them. An important point is that an MP is not a delegate, bound by the views of his constituents, rather a representative who takes account of their views, but who, at the end of the day, exercises his own judgement.

Forming Governments

In the two-party Westminster system, the majority party provides, mostly from the House of Commons, the members of the UK Cabinet, the Ministers of the Crown and unpaid Parliamentary Private Secretaries. The Opposition party in the UK Parliament is intended to be a Government in waiting. It has a Shadow Cabinet and various other MPs as opposition spokespersons. Organising support within the House of Commons is the job of the Whips. By means of persuasion, political bribery or threats, the Whips organise MPs' support for their respective party groups.

Legislative

Parliamentary legislation is mainly initiated by the Government and tends to introduce changes to society which reflect the policies of a particular Government. Proposals for an Act of Parliament take the form of a Bill and, during the opening ceremony of Parliament, the Queen will generally outline the forthcoming Bills for the year ahead. Bills themselves fall into three distinct categories. *Public Bills* are the most important and take up the majority of parliamentary time since they deal with matters of important principle and generally affect society as a whole.

There are two types of Public Bill: Government Bills and Private Members' Bills. Government Bills are introduced by the ruling Government of the day and generally reflect current policy or manifesto commitments. For example, the Constitutional Reform Act 2005 was introduced as a Government Bill reflecting the Labour Government's enthusiasm for judicial reform. The majority of Acts passed by Parliament originate from Government Bills; Private Members' Bills, on the other hand, generally originate from an individual MP. These Bills will more often than not deal with an area which does not receive Government backing or is controversial, and they often reflect personally held beliefs of MPs. In some cases, controversial measures for which a Government does not want to take responsibility may be introduced by back-benchers, with the Government secretly or openly backing the measure and ensuring its passage. Such Bills are sometimes known as "Government handout Bills"; the Abortion Act 1967 was passed in such a manner. This type of Bill ensures that back-benchers have more input into the legislative process of Parliament but the success of such Bills is very limited. Most Private Members' Bills fail to become Acts.

The second category of Bills is known as *Private Bills*. These contain proposals which generally affect the interests of specified persons or localities. They are introduced through petition by the persons or organisations who desire the Bill. Private Bills are commonly introduced by local authorities or public corporations and seek to give statutory powers to those bodies which they would otherwise not have. For example, the Transport for London Bill is currently before Parliament and seeks to give the London Assembly and the Greater London Authority increased powers relating to the regulation of transport. Private Bills follow a slightly different procedure in their enactment from other Bills and there is often very little discussion of such Bills within Parliament.

The third and final category of Bills is called *Hybrid Bills*. These are usually Government Bills which specifically affect particular individuals or groups. They are therefore treated in many ways like Private Bills. An example of such a Bill can be found in the Channel Tunnel Bill of 1986, now the Channel Tunnel Act 1987. The Bill was generally Public in nature, given that it set out to create the Channel Tunnel, however, certain sections of the Act gave the Government powers of compulsory purchase to buy areas of land in Kent required to build the Tunnel. Since these sections specifically affected only Kent landowners, the Bill was Hybrid in nature.

Parliamentary stages of Bills

Bills may be introduced in either the House of Commons or the House of Lords. However, there are a number of Bills which must always originate in the Commons, such as Money Bills and Bills of constitutional importance.

A Bill which originates in the House of Lords will progress through the same stages as those in the House of Commons. The stages of a Bill as it passes through Parliament are as follows:

- **First Reading**

  The first stage consists of a number of formalities where the Bill is announced and its short title is read out. A date is set for the Second Reading of the Bill and from here the Bill will be printed and distributed.

- **Second Reading**

  At this stage, the House will debate the general principles contained in the Bill. At the end of the debate, the motion is put to a vote. It is very rare for a Government Bill to lose a vote, although it is not unheard of. For example, the Shops Bill 1986 was lost at the Second Reading.

- **Committee Stage**

  During the Committee Stage, most Bills are passed over to a Standing Committee which is created for the specific purpose of dealing with the Bill. Standing Committees generally consist of between 18 and 50 MPs and reflect the state of the parties represented in the House of Commons. At this stage, the Bill is subjected to a thorough line-by-line examination and any of its clauses may be amended where necessary.

  A small number of Bills at this stage are passed over to a Committee of the Whole House as opposed to a Standing Committee. During such a Committee, each clause of the Bill is debated on the floor of the House of Commons by all MPs. Such a Committee is used for Bills of constitutional significance, such as the Scotland Bill during 1999. It is also used to pass Bills which require a rapid enactment, such as the annual Finance Bill.

- **Report Stage**

  If a Bill has come from a Committee of the Whole House, then this stage is purely a formality. However, for the majority of Bills, this stage will involve a review of any amendments made during the Committee Stage. All members of the House have an opportunity to debate at this stage, making it rather more democratic than the Committee stage where the scope for debate is rather limited. There is no vote at this point.

- **Third Reading**

  Here, the House examines the final version of the Bill. The Bill is debated in principle and a vote taken. This stage is usually very brief, since no major amendments may be made.

A key problem with the legislative process of the Commons is the amount of time it takes. The more amendments a Bill receives, the longer it will take to pass through Parliament. Consequently, many Bills are subject to what is called a "guillotine" motion. Such a motion will quickly bring the debate on a Bill to an end, allowing it to proceed more quickly. Since 1999, the Commons has also used a new procedure known as the "programme" motion. Using this motion, a programme or timetable is put before the House, agreeing the amount of time allocated to stages of a Bill and dates for progression.

- **Lords Stages**

  Once the Commons stages have been completed, the Bill is sent to the House of Lords where the whole procedure is repeated. The Lords Stages are similar in many ways to those of the Commons, except for a few key differences. The Committee Stage in the Lords always consists of a Committee of the Whole House and there is no use of guillotine or programme motions, which allows for unrestricted debate on the principles of a Bill. It is also possible to table amendments during the Third Reading in the Lords.

  Changes made to a Bill in the House of Lords result in an extra stage in the Commons, known as Lords Amendments Considered. This is necessary in order to approve any amendments made by the Lords. Occasionally, the two Houses will not agree on a Bill. In such circumstances, the Lords can exercise its delaying power and refuse to accept the proposals of the House of Commons. However, this delaying power is limited by the Parliament Act 1911, as amended by the Parliament Act 1949 which states that the Lords can delay a Bill only for up to 1 year. Using the Parliament Acts, the House of Commons can then submit a Bill for Royal Assent without the consent of the House of Lords. Thus, the power of the House of Lords to block legislation permanently is curtailed. Unless the House of Commons invokes the Parliament Acts, then both Houses of Parliament must always agree in order for the final Bill to progress.

- **Royal Assent**

  This is the final stage of a Bill, where the Crown must formally assent to the Bill in order for it to become an Act of Parliament and pass into law. In modern times this has become something of a formality since the UK is a constitutional monarchy and the sovereign is bound to assent to any Bill, except in extraordinary circumstances. The last time assent was given by the Crown in person was in 1854 and assent has not been refused since 1707, when Queen Anne refused to consent to the Scottish Militia Bill.

Scrutiny of the executive

The Government's responsibility to Parliament for its actions is promoted and enforced by way of a number of procedural and legal mechanisms. These primarily take the form of debates, questions, committees and the Parliamentary Commissioner for Administration. The role of the Parliamentary Commissioner in holding government to account for its actions is discussed fully in Chapter 11.

Debates

There are many opportunities for debate within the House, the main ones being:

- **Address in reply to the Queen's Speech**

  An address in answer is moved in both Houses of Parliament. It is moved and seconded by two members of the majority party, in the form of a resolution expressing thanks to the Sovereign for her most gracious speech. Amendments are moved thereto. The debate may last several days and covers the whole range of government policy, especially in relation to the Queen's Speech.

- **Opposition Day debates**

  Standing Order 14 of the House of Commons Standing Orders provides that on 20 days in each session, proceedings on business chosen by the Opposition parties shall have precedence over Government business. Seventeen of the days are allocated to the disposal of the Leader of the Opposition. The remaining three days are at the disposal of the second-largest party of Opposition, ie the party which has the second-largest number of members elected to the House. Two of the seventeen and one of the three days can be taken as half-days (not on a Friday) to allow the Opposition the opportunity of raising urgent matters at short notice.

- **Adjournment debates**

  At the conclusion of public business each day, a member of the Government may move an adjournment debate. Members must put their names down in advance, with ballots being held for the adjournment debates on Monday, Tuesday, Wednesday and Friday. The subject for Thursday is selected by the Speaker of the House. Adjournment debates are unlikely to make any significant impact, since Ministers are given adequate notice, thus allowing them to prepare their responses.

- **Emergency debates**

  Members have an opportunity to move the adjournment of the House for discussion of a specific matter requiring urgent consideration. The member must inform the Speaker of his intention and leave of the House must be given. The motion usually stands over until the commencement of public business the next day or, if sufficiently urgent, until 7 pm on that day.

Questions

Parliamentary questions are raised during every sitting day, except Friday. Such questions are popular and around 50,000 are set down for every parliamentary session. There are a number of key reasons for asking parliamentary questions:

(1) to raise constituency matters (though this is normally done by letter to a Minister);

(2) to extract information – for example, "How many Acts of Parliament have been passed since 1999 utilising a Sewell Motion?";

(3) to advocate a cause;

(4) to embarrass the Government or the Minister; and

(5) to offer a Minister the chance to make a policy statement.

Generally, answers given are in response to prior written questions. A written answer is normally given within one working week and printed in the Official Report (*Hansard*). However, an MP may raise supplementary oral questions based upon a Minister's reply, for which no formal notice is required. This provides a good opportunity to place Ministers on the spot regarding key issues.

It is central to the rules governing parliamentary questions that questions should relate to matters for which Ministers are responsible. In July 1999, following the establishment of the Scottish Parliament and the National Assembly for Wales, various matters became the responsibility of Ministers answerable to those bodies. The Commons Procedure Committee recommended that the rules on questions should be revised to take account of devolution, and on 25 October 1999 the House approved a motion on this subject. The effect of the resolution is that, in general, parliamentary questions may not be tabled at Westminster on matters that have been devolved to Scotland and Wales.

House of Commons Committees

Not all of an MP's time is spent in the debating chamber. Much of the work of the House of Commons is carried on through parliamentary committees which include Select Committees, Public Bill and General Committees, and other specialised committees such as the Ecclesiastical Committee. Each provides powerful opportunities for scrutinising the work of the executive.

Select Committees

Generally speaking, Select Committees play the most important role in scrutinising the executive, and they frequently influence and modify aspects of policy. Such committees were originally ad hoc, ie set up to investigate a particular issue; however, some took on a quasi-permanent nature and were re-appointed in consecutive sessions, such as the Public Accounts Committee. From 1967 onwards, a limited number of specialist Select Committees were set up, in an attempt to improve the efficiency of the House in scrutinising the conduct of the administration. It began with the Committee on Agriculture and the Committee on Science and Technology; followed by Scottish Affairs, Race Relations, Immigration and Overseas Development. These committees were able to build up a body of specialist knowledge and increase the effectiveness of their scrutiny of the executive.

In 1978, the Select Committee on Procedure recommended a re-organisation of the structure to provide scrutiny on "a continuing and systematic basis". This was to be achieved by basing each committee on a government department, instead of on specific subjects. Thus, the modern system of departmental Select Committees was established in June 1979. They are charged with examining all aspects of expenditure, administration and policy and are appointed for the lifetime of each Parliament, not just a session. For a list of the current committees, see http://www.parliament. uk/parliamentary_committees/parliamentary_committees16.cfm.

Select Committees have a minimum of 11 members who reflect the party balance in the House of Commons. They decide upon the line of inquiry and then gather written and oral evidence. Findings are reported to the Commons, printed and published on the Parliament website. The Government then usually has 60 days to reply to the committee's recommendations. Overall, these committees provide a forum in which Ministers, civil servants and others can be cross-examined at length and thoroughly. They usually produce unanimous reports which cross party lines and present powerful all-party criticism of the Government. Unfortunately, however, the House of Commons rarely finds time for substantive debate of the reports.

Joint Committees

Joint Committees operate in a similar fashion to Select Committees; however, they consist of equal numbers of members of the House of Commons and House of Lords. They are appointed at the insistence of one House or the other, on an ad hoc basis. However, two Joint Committees meet on a regular basis: Human Rights, which meets to consider UK human rights issues; and Statutory Instruments, which scrutinises delegated legislation.

THE HOUSE OF LORDS

The United Kingdom has a bicameral legislature, ie one consisting of two Houses (the House of Commons and the House of Lords). The House of Lords is known as the "Upper House" of the UK Parliament, in reference to its historical position which was one of superior political power. This power has gradually been eroded and the role of the Lords today is to act as a second chamber for revising legislation, and to complement the work of the House of Commons. The House of Lords is also the highest court of appeal in the UK, although this function will soon be moved to the new Supreme Court of the United Kingdom by virtue of the Constitutional Reform Act 2005.

Composition

Until 1999, the House of Lords had 1,330 members, the majority of whom were hereditary peers who had inherited their peerages. Under the House of Lords Act 1999, most of the hereditary peers lost their right to sit in the House of Lords. The current membership (as of May 2007) of the House is 731 who fall into a number of distinct groupings:

(1) the Lords Spiritual;

(2) hereditary peers;

(3) the Lords of Appeal in Ordinary; and

(4) life peers.

The Lords Spiritual

The Anglican Archbishops of Canterbury and York, the Bishops of Durham, London and Winchester, and the 21 senior diocesan bishops of the Church of England have seats in the House. Only the Church of England is represented officially, even though the Church of Scotland is an established Church too. This is because the Church of England is the "established" Church of the State. When a Lord Spiritual retires as a bishop, his membership of the House ceases.

Hereditary peers

Hereditary peers were historically the least legitimate element of the House of Lords, since their peerages were simply inherited. Many campaigners queried the right of such individuals to sit and vote in Parliament by virtue of birth and in 1999 the Government finally decided to abolish hereditary peers from the second chamber. Until the passing of the House of Lords Act 1999 there had been around 700 hereditary members; however, there are now only 92. They are the result of an amendment which was made to the House of Lords Bill, enabling the exemption of 92 existing hereditary peers. These peers will remain as members until the next stage of reform and are made up as follows:

- 15 "office-holders", ie Deputy Speakers and Deputy Chairmen, elected by the House;
- 75 party and cross-bench members elected by their own party or group; and
- two who hold royal appointments: the Lord Great Chamberlain, who is the Queen's representative in Parliament; and the Earl Marshal, who is responsible for ceremonies such as the State Opening of Parliament.

The Lords of Appeal in Ordinary

In the middle of the 19th century, attention was drawn to the fact that there was a dearth of qualified lawyers in the House of Lords. This was particularly unfortunate since the House of Lords is the highest court of appeal in the UK (subject to reform when the provisions of the Constitutional Reform Act 2005 come fully into force). This situation led to the passing of the Appellate Jurisdiction Act 1876 under which two Lords of Appeal in Ordinary were introduced. The number has gradually risen to allow up to 12 Law Lords to be appointed to hear appeals from the lower courts. They are salaried senior judges and can continue to hear appeals until they are 70 years old. After they retire, they go on sitting in the House. However, the judicial function of the House of Lords will end in October 2009 when the new Supreme Court of the United Kingdom is set up under the Constitutional Reform Act 2005. As a result, the Law Lords will lose their right to sit in the House of Lords.

Life peers

The Life Peerages Act 1958 enables the Sovereign to confer a barony for life, carrying the right to sit in the House of Lords. There is no limit to the number and life peers currently make up the majority (about 600) of the total membership of the House. Although the power to appoint belongs formally to the Crown, members are essentially created on the advice of the Prime Minister. They play a very significant part in the work of the House of Lords and serve to secure the experience and wisdom of citizens from all walks of life. Once a year or so, a list of new working peers is drawn up by the Prime Minister after consultation with the leaders of the Opposition parties.

Functions

The House of Lords has a number of key functions:

- it provides a forum for debate on issues of public interest;
- it acts as the revising chamber for Bills introduced in the House of Commons;
- it can initiate Public Bills, generally less controversial ones, and Private Members' Bills;
- it scrutinises subordinate legislation and private legislation;
- it scrutinises European Union proposals;
- it scrutinises the activities of the executive; and
- it is the Supreme Court of Appeal for England and Wales, and also for Scottish civil cases (subject to reform when the provisions of the Constitutional Reform Act 2005 come fully into force).

Members of the House are not paid in the carrying out of its functions (other than a small number of Members who are salaried by virtue of the office they hold). Members can, however, be reimbursed for travel, subsistence and office costs incurred in connection with their parliamentary duties. The allowances are based on recommendations of the Senior Salaries Review Body and the daily maxima from 1 August 2006 to 31 July 2007 are £159.50 for travel; £79.50 for subsistence; and £69 for office costs. Members' expenses amount to only 15 per cent of the annual running costs of the House of Lords. For a detailed overview

of the annual financing of the House, see http://www.parliament.uk/
documents/upload/HofbpFinancing.pdf.

Powers

Up until 1911, the Lords and the Commons had the same legislative powers,
except in money matters. By convention, Bills dealing with taxation or
public expenditure had to be introduced in the House of Commons and
could not be amended by the House of Lords, although the Lords had the
formal right to reject them completely. The convention was that where the
will of the people was behind the House of Commons, the Lords should
give way. Between 1906 and 1909, the Lords rejected several important
measures proposed by the Liberal Government, including, in 1909, the
Government's Finance Bill. This led to the Lords' power of veto being
reduced to one of delay for a period of 2 years under the Parliament Act
1911. This was further reduced to 1 year by the Parliament Act 1949 which
arose from a disagreement between the House of Lords and the Labour
Government over nationalisation of coal and steel.

The effect of the Parliament Acts means that certain Acts of Parliament
can be passed without the consent of the House of Lords. The 1949
Act itself was passed under the provisions of the 1911 Act, ie without
the consent of the House of Lords. Very few Bills have been enacted
in this way, since most differences are usually resolved by compromise.
However, recent examples passed using the procedure include the
European Parliamentary Elections Act 1999 and the Hunting Act 2004.
Some constitutional academics are of the opinion that the 1949 Act is not
a proper Act of Parliament, but a special kind of delegated legislation and
so Acts passed using the 1949 procedure could be challenged as to their
validity. However, this argument now appears to have been discredited by
the decision in *Jackson* v *Attorney-General* (2005).

The procedures of the Parliament Acts cannot be used to extend the
life of a Parliament beyond 5 years, nor do they apply to Private Bills,
subordinate legislation or Bills which start in the House of Lords.

Future reform

The House of Lords Act 1999 was intended to be "stage one" of a series of
reforms aimed at making the upper chamber more democratic. The Labour
Government was elected in 1997 with a commitment to reform the House
of Lords, principally through the removal of hereditary peers, prior to a
second stage of reform. In early 1999, the Government published a White
Paper on House of Lords reform, entitled *Modernising Parliament, Reforming*

the House of Lords (Cm 4183, 1999) and established a Royal Commission chaired by former Conservative Cabinet Minister Lord Wakeham (the Wakeham Commission) to produce a proposal for a wholly reconstituted second chamber.

The Wakeham Commission

The Royal Commission reported in January 2000. Entitled *A House for the Future* (Cm 4534), the report was far-reaching in its proposals and provided a blueprint for a wholly reconstituted second chamber. Among its key recommendations were that an appointments system should be set up. This would be governed by a body known as the Appointments Commission. It would be independent of the Prime Minister, the Government and the political parties and would be responsible for all appointments to the second chamber. The Commission would have a number of duties which would include ensuring gender balance, appointing a significant number of regional members and the maintenance of a political balance. The Wakeham Commission also suggested that the existing life peers, who were created before the publication of the Commission's findings, should be deemed to have been appointed to the reformed second chamber for life. However, any life peers created between publication and the enactment of any legislation necessary to implement the second stage of Lords reforms should be deemed to have been appointed to the reformed second chamber for a period of only 15 years from the award of their life peerages.

Events since Wakeham

In May 2000, the Government established an independent non-statutory Appointments Commission with a number of key functions:

- to recommend people for appointment as non-party-political life peers;
- to vet all nominations for membership of the House of Lords, including those nominated by the political parties; and
- to scrutinise certain candidates added to the Honours lists.

However, from this point on, reform of the House of Lords has remained unfinished business despite the 2005 manifestos of the three main parties being committed to further reform. The lack of progress has been rooted in the fact that the Government has been unable to agree on a specific template for the new second chamber. Despite widespread party commitment for change, there are strongly held and conflicting views on particular aspects of reform. An area of particular contention has been that of membership of the House. Many MPs advocate a wholly elected second chamber to add democratric legitimacy, while opponents prefer only a partially elected House.

In an attempt to move forward, a "Breaking the Deadlock" group was formed in 2005 and a Cross-Party Working Group on Lords Reform in 2006. The work of these groups has culminated in the issuing of a White Paper entitled *The House of Lords: Reform* (2007). In the Government's view, it is difficult, in a modern democracy, to justify a second chamber where there is no elected element. The White Paper therefore proposes that a reformed House should be a hybrid House, ie partially appointed and elected. Opinions as to the balance between the elected and appointed members have, however, varied. The White Paper suggests a model whereby 50 per cent of the House is elected through a partially open list system, with elections being held at the same time as elections to the European Parliament and using the same constituencies. The appointed element of the House would continue through a new Statutory Appointments Commission. At the time of writing (May 2007), a free vote in the House of Commons has led to the proposal that the reformed upper chamber should be 80 per cent elected. It is likely that a draft Bill will be introduced to Parliament during the course of 2007. It is envisaged that the final stage of reform will take some time since there will be a long period of transition within which existing life peers will not be forced to leave. However, the right of the remaining hereditary peers to sit in the House will finally be brought to an end.

Abolition?

Although some academics have argued for abolition of the House of Lords, it is doubtful whether a policy of outright abolition would take adequate account of the special dangers that that could pose in the uncodified British constitution. With a unicameral legislature and no entrenched procedures for constitutional change, it would be legally possible for extreme changes to be brought about by one vote. The implications of abolition would be far-reaching, given the vagaries of our present electoral system which usually produces a Government with a significant majority.

PARLIAMENTARY PRIVILEGE

Parliamentary privilege is part of the law and custom of Parliament and refers to the freedom of each House to conduct its proceedings without interference from the Crown, courts, external bodies or the public. It consists of special rules evolved by the two Houses to protect themselves collectively, and their members individually, while acting in their public capacity. Their existence and validity are recognised by the courts but in general they are not enforced by the courts but by each House. The key privileges relate to:

- freedom of speech and debate;
- freedom from arrest;
- the right to regulate composition;
- the right to regulate proceedings; and
- the right to punish for breach of privilege or for contempt.

Freedom of speech and debate

Article 9 of the Bill of Rights 1688 states that freedom of speech and debates or proceedings in Parliament ought not to be impeached or questioned in any court or place out of Parliament. Originally, this was aimed at protecting members from the king if they criticised him. Today, however, it has a very different significance, namely to protect members from actions of damages for statements made in Parliament. The effect in law is that no criminal or civil action can be brought against a member for words used in Parliament, no matter how defamatory or untrue they are. Furthermore, a member cannot be threatened with prosecution for sedition or breach of the Official Secrets Acts. In *Duncan Sandys' Case* (1938), Sandys complained that he had been threatened with prosecution for refusing to divulge his sources of information obtained in breach of the Official Secrets Act in connection with a parliamentary question he had tabled about a shortage of anti-aircraft material. The law of privilege protected Sandys from prosecution.

There are certain things which cannot be said in the House, such as "liar", but it is Parliament itself, not the courts, which has the power to discipline MPs. Not only can no action of defamation be brought in respect of anything said in the House, neither can what has been said there be examined in court for the purpose of deciding whether the statement supports an action in defamation which has arisen outside Parliament. In *Church of Scientology of California* v *Johnson-Smith* (1972), Johnson-Smith, MP was alleged to have published a libel during a TV interview about the Church. He had previously asked a question of the Minister of Health in the House of Commons, which resulted in alien scientologists being refused admission to the UK. The Church sought to rebut Johnson-Smith's plea of fair comment by referring to proceedings in Parliament, recorded in *Hansard*. The High Court held that parliamentary privilege meant that they could not examine these proceedings in court.

This does not mean, however, that no reference at all can be made to parliamentary proceedings in court. In *Pepper v Hart* (1993), it was argued that the use of *Hansard* for the purpose of statutory interpretation would constitute a questioning of the freedom of speech or debate, contrary to Art 9 of the Bill of Rights 1688. The House of Lords disagreed and stated that, far from questioning the independence of Parliament and its debates, the use by courts of clear ministerial statements as a guide to construction of ambiguous legislation would help to give effect to what is said and done in Parliament.

There is one important qualification in this area, namely that parliamentary privilege only extends to statements made during proceedings in Parliament. Thus, the courts may intervene if a member defames someone outside Parliament. This has led to difficulties due to the imprecise meaning of "proceedings" in Parliament. It has been said to extend to asking parliamentary questions, to everything said or done by a member in the exercise of functions in committees, and to conversations between MPs and Ministers in a Minister's office. A particular problem which has arisen is the question of whether a letter from an MP to a Minister is a proceeding in Parliament. In *Re Parliamentary Privilege Act 1770* (1958), George Strauss, MP wrote to a Minister, complaining about certain activities of an area electricity board. The board threatened to sue Strauss for libel. Strauss raised the matter in the House and it was referred to the Committee of Privileges which held that writing the letter was a proceeding in Parliament and that the board was in breach of parliamentary privilege. The House debated the committee's report and, on a free vote, rejected the committee's finding that it was a proceeding in Parliament. Thus, the protection afforded is not total. However, the Speaker later indicated that parliamentary privilege would extend to a letter written by an MP to a Minister in response to an invitation to do so made during a parliamentary debate or in response to a question.

Following the decision in *Stockdale v Hansard* (1839), the Parliamentary Papers Act 1840 was passed which confers absolute privilege on statements in parliamentary papers. Qualified privilege applies to publications of fair and accurate reports of parliamentary papers.

Freedom from arrest

This was enjoyed by the MPs of both the Scottish and English Parliaments to protect them from the king. The privilege is of little importance now, and in 1967 the Committee on Parliamentary Privilege recommended its abolition. The privilege lasts for a session of Parliament and for 40 days before and after it. It does not protect members from arrest on criminal charges. A warrant for the arrest of Ron Brown, MP was issued in 1988, for criminal damage to the Commons' mace. He was found guilty of criminal damage.

The privilege does protect from civil arrest (although this is very rare now). In *Stourton* v *Stourton* (1963), Stourton, a peer, failed to comply with a court order regarding maintenance for his wife. He pleaded freedom from arrest under parliamentary privilege. The court concluded that parliamentary privilege existed in relation to the civil law and so Stourton was protected.

Right to regulate composition

This area is now partly regulated by statute and the privilege covers:

- filling casual vacancies;
- determining disputed elections;
- determining legal disqualifications; and
- expulsion of members unfit to serve.

Right to regulate proceedings

This rule is closely linked with the rule that proceedings in Parliament cannot be called into question in any court. The privilege is quite strictly followed and is the reason why the courts will not question the procedural validity of an Act of Parliament (*Pickin* v *British Railways Board* (1974)). Similarly, in *Bradlaugh* v *Gossett* (1884), Bradlaugh, a militant atheist, refused to take the oath of allegiance on being elected as an MP. Eventually, the House of Commons reluctantly allowed him to affirm his allegiance. However, an action was brought against him on the grounds that he had sat and voted without taking the oath, and that he did not come within the classes of persons entitled to affirm, and so his seat was declared vacant. Bradlaugh was subsequently re-elected and the House of Commons sought to exclude him. Bradlaugh raised an action seeking an injunction to prevent the Serjeant-at-Arms (Gossett) from excluding him. The court held that it had no jurisdiction to intervene. The House was not subject to control by the courts in its administration of internal proceedings.

Theft, rape, murder or other serious crimes are issues to be left to the criminal courts. The penal powers of the House are not adequate to deal with crimes. If two members assault each other in the House, both the House and the courts have concurrent jurisdiction. However, in 1972, when Bernadette Devlin, MP assaulted the Home Secretary, Reginald Maudling, pulled his hair and knocked his spectacles off, no proceedings were taken against her, either inside or outside the House.

When in doubt, the courts tread warily, for fear of encroaching on the House's privileges. In *R v Graham-Campbell, ex parte Herbert* (1935), Herbert wanted to liberalise licensing laws. He tried to embarrass the House of Commons' Kitchen Committee members by applying for a summons against them for selling alcohol in the House of Commons bar without a licence. The Divisional Court upheld the decision of the Chief Magistrate to refuse to issue a summons because of parliamentary privilege. Additionally, licensing laws do not bind the Crown, and the House of Commons is part of the Royal Palace of Westminster.

Right to punish for breach of privilege or for contempt

All breaches of privilege are contempts, but a wide range of contempts fall outside the scope of any named privilege. Examples of contempts include: offering bribes to members; molesting or obstructing members or officers of the Houses; insulting the House or its members; attempting to disrupt proceedings; refusing to give evidence to a committee; and intimidation of members.

Punishments

(i) *Expulsion*: leads to a vacancy, but the House cannot prevent re-election. Garry Allighan, MP was expelled in 1947, for lying to a committee and for gross contempt of the House after publication of an article in the *World's Press News* accusing Members of insobriety and of taking fees or bribes for the supply of information.

(ii) *Suspension for a temporary period*: in 1995, the Conservative MPs Graham Riddick and David Tredinnick were formally reprimanded and suspended without pay by the House of Commons for 10 and 20 sitting days respectively, for taking £1,000 to ask questions in the House of Commons (see HC Debates, vol 258, no 59, cols 350 *et seq*).

(iii) *Imprisonment of a member; imprisonment of a stranger in Her Majesty's Prison*: this has not been used since the 1880s, and the Committee of Privileges has recommended that this power should be abolished.

(iv) *Reprimand*: the Speaker addresses the offender, either standing in his place (Member) or at the bar of the House. In the "cash for questions" scandal of recent times, Peter Preston, the editor of *The Guardian*, was summoned before the bar of the Commons. He had authorised the use of a fake fax on Commons' headed paper, purporting to come from the office of Jonathan Aitken, MP, to get a copy of the MP's bill for a two-night stay at the Ritz Hotel in Paris.

(v) *Admonition*: milder than the above, but administered in the same way.

(vi) *Fines*: not used by the House of Commons since 1666, though the Select Committee in 1967 recommended that this be revived by statute. The House of Lords, as a court of record (it is uncertain whether the House of Commons is such), has frequently imposed fines.

Essential Facts

- The UK Parliament consists of the monarch, the House of Commons and the House of Lords.
- The maximum life of a UK Parliament is 5 years.
- An Act of Parliament usually requires the consent of the House of Commons and the House of Lords, and the assent of the monarch.
- Acts of Parliament may be passed without the consent of the House of Lords, utilising the Parliament Acts of 1911 and 1949.
- Most residents of the UK aged 18 years or over are entitled to vote in UK elections.
- Most residents aged 21 years or over are entitled to stand for election to the UK Parliament. The Parliament is elected using the "first past the post" electoral system.
- Important functions of Parliament include the passing of laws, scrutiny of the executive and the control of taxation and expenditure.
- Parliamentary privilege is part of the law and custom of Parliament and refers to the freedom of each House to conduct its proceedings without interference from the Crown, courts, external bodies or the public.

Essential Cases

Jackson v Attorney-General (2005): concerned the validity of an Act of Parliament passed using the procedures of the Parliament Acts 1911 and 1949.

Duncan Sandys' Case (1938): concerned the protection of freedom of speech and debate in Parliament by the law of privilege.

Pepper v Hart (1993): held that the use of *Hansard* as an aid to statutory interpretation was permitted.

Stourton v Stourton (1963): held that the law of parliamentary privilege will extend to protect members of Parliament from civil proceedings.

Bradlaugh v Gossett (1884): held that the House of Commons was not subject to control by the courts in its administration of internal proceedings.

7 THE UNITED KINGDOM GOVERNMENT

The Government of the United Kingdom consists of the monarch, the Prime Minister, the Cabinet and other Ministers of the Crown. The Queen is the titular head of the Government and all actions of government are carried out in her name. Her role, however, is largely a formal one and the position of the monarch has already been discussed fully in Chapter 5.

THE PRIME MINISTER AND THE CABINET

There are many areas in public law where law and politics become entwined and none more so than in relation to the Prime Minister and the Cabinet. There are relatively few statutes and precious little case authority which refer to either the Cabinet or the Prime Minister. As a result, the rules governing each institution are not, in the main, rules of strict law but derive from political conventions and usage. The Cabinet and the office of Prime Minister have evolved together since the 18th century and the decline of the Privy Council seems to have coincided with the emergence of the Cabinet. In 1713, the Treaty of Utrecht was concluded by the Cabinet, not by the Privy Council, and in 1714 George I acceded to the throne. He was a Hanoverian with little interest in Britain and his attendances at Cabinet became less and less frequent until they finally stopped altogether. Thus, someone else had to preside in place of the monarch and it is accepted that Sir Robert Walpole (1721–42), when First Lord of the Treasury under Georges I and II, became the first Prime Minister. However, many historians doubt that anyone prior to Sir Robert Peel (1841–46) would count as the first modern Prime Minister. By that time, some of the important conventions of the Cabinet were becoming firmly established.

The Prime Minister

Appointment

As we have seen when dealing with the personal prerogatives of the monarch in Chapter 5, the Queen, by convention, invites the leader of the political party which wins the largest number of seats at a General Election to form a Government. Since all the major political parties now elect their own leaders, the monarch has little discretion here. Although in the past there have been Prime Ministers who were members of the House of Lords, today, the Prime Minister must, by convention, be a member of the House of Commons.

Experience

Prime Ministers are experienced party politicians and will usually have held previous ministerial office. Previous Prime Ministers have averaged over 20 years' membership in Parliament before becoming Prime Minister. However, the recently outgoing Prime Minister, Tony Blair, did not hold ministerial office prior to assuming the premiership on 2 May 1997 (his previous 14 years in Parliament had been spent in Opposition).

Convention now requires the Prime Minister to be a member of the House of Commons. In 1963, when the Earl of Home emerged as the favoured successor to Harold Macmillan and was invited to become Prime Minister, he renounced his peerage and became "plain" Sir Alec Douglas-Home. Apart from Douglas-Home, no Prime Minister since Lord Salisbury in 1902 has come from the House of Lords.

Joint offices

For most of its history, the office of Prime Minister has been held along with a recognised post, usually the First Lord of the Treasury (the Second being the Chancellor of the Exchequer). When the Civil Service Department was established in 1968, the Prime Minister also became the Minister for the Civil Service.

Pay and conditions

The Prime Minister has official residences in Downing Street and at Chequers and is paid and pensioned under the Ministerial and Other Salaries Act 1975 and the Ministerial and Other Pensions and Salaries Act 1991. The Prime Minister's pay consists of two elements: the parliamentary salary (Members' pay) and a ministerial salary. The combined salary entitlement for the Prime Minister from 1 November 2006 has been £187,611.

Powers of the Prime Minister

The appointment or dismissal of Ministers

The monarch has nominal powers of appointment and dismissal but these are exercised on the advice of the Prime Minister. There are no legal or conventional restraints on the Prime Minister's choice of Ministers, although there are political considerations to be taken into account. The monopoly of appointment augments the power of the Prime Minister over back-benchers and junior Ministers.

The appointment of Cabinet Ministers

By convention or custom, certain Ministers are always included in a peace-time Cabinet: the Chancellor of the Exchequer, Foreign Secretary, Home Secretary, Secretary of State for Scotland, Leader of the House of Commons, Lord Chancellor and heads of major spending departments. This limits the Prime Minister's freedom of choice, but he can re-shuffle, promote or dismiss at will. The Prime Minister can use this power to maintain discipline and increase Prime Ministerial power. The Queen dismisses on the Prime Minister's advice and it is not clear whether there are any circumstances in which she could refuse. It would appear that the Prime Minister's resignation alone requires the resignation of all other Ministers, as in 1990, with the resignation of Margaret Thatcher.

Control over the machinery of government

The Prime Minister decides on the allocation of tasks to different government departments and whether departments should be created, amalgamated, re-named or abolished. In 1997, the Department of National Heritage, created by John Major in 1992, was re-named the Department of Culture, Sport and the Media by Tony Blair. Similarly, a "super-Ministry", the Department of the Environment, Transport and the Regions, was created in 1997 from an amalgamation of the old Departments of Transport and of the Environment.

Control over the Cabinet

The Prime Minister controls the agenda, chairs the meetings and sums up Cabinet discussions. He also decides which Cabinet committees should be established, who should chair them and who will serve on them (although the Prime Minister will chair important Cabinet committees directly). It is also the case that a Prime Minister may make major decisions without reference to the Cabinet, either personally or in consultation with senior colleagues. Finally, the Prime Minister communicates Cabinet decisions to the monarch and discusses affairs of state with her in a weekly audience.

Dissolution of Parliament

The Prime Minister alone advises the monarch on the dissolution of Parliament, although he may consult senior colleagues about the timing of such a dissolution. This power enhances the authority of the Prime Minister over MPs, parties and the country as a whole.

Powers of patronage

Appointments to archbishoprics, to high judicial office and to high military office are expected to be made on a non-political basis and leave the Prime Minister with little discretion. But with others, the Prime Minister's discretion is real and those in line for appointment may be less inclined to be critical of the Prime Minister. Peerages, knighthoods and other honours, and the chairmanship of a quango, Royal Commission or public inquiry have all been in the gift of the Prime Minister at one time or another, through his nomination and/or advice to the Queen.

Policy co-ordination

No other Minister has the same information and resources at his disposal as the Prime Minster who can intervene with impunity in what is substantively another Minister's area of responsibility, as Margaret Thatcher often did. Sometimes this is done through a co-ordinating Minister in the Cabinet Office, eg David Hunt and latterly Michael Heseltine for John Major, and Jack Cunningham (from July 1998 onwards) for Tony Blair. The Prime Minister normally takes a close interest in EU and other foreign affairs as well as economic policy. The recently outgoing Prime Minister Tony Blair took a particular interest in education matters.

Constitutional implications of the Prime Minister's powers

In theory, a Prime Minister is *primus inter pares* (first among equals) but a strong individual can dominate the Cabinet and exert overwhelming levels of authority. There is always a danger that a Prime Minister becomes almost dictatorial and is eager to exert control over all aspects of government. This was especially self-evident during the tenure of Margaret Thatcher. However, it is worth noting that when a Prime Minster becomes over-zealous, then they run the danger of losing the respect and support of their senior colleagues. Mrs Thatcher, who lost the confidence of her senior colleagues and many of her party, was dealt with by the Conservatives' internal party machinery, including the "men in grey suits", and eventually resigned in November 1990.

The Cabinet

The Cabinet is the name given to a special committee of senior Ministers who are responsible for making and controlling government policy. They meet every Thursday morning at the Cabinet Room in 10 Downing Street to discuss the issues of the day. Like the Prime Minister, the Cabinet is almost invisible in statute law. As an organ of government, it rests on convention and there is no statute or common law rule as to its composition or powers. The Cabinet in Parliament is the central feature of the British constitution. It is the collective leadership of the majority party in the House of Commons and, through its control of that party, the Cabinet exercises control over Parliament.

A modern Cabinet consists of 18–24 members and in normal circumstances is politically homogeneous, ie all Conservative or Labour, and its members must be members of the House of Lords or House of Commons. There are some political and administrative constraints on the Prime Minister's choice of Cabinet members. As mentioned above, certain Ministers have to be included and there is perhaps also a tradition or convention arising that a woman should be included in the Cabinet. There was something of an outcry when John Major did not have a woman in his first Cabinet in November 1990. He appointed two women to his second, following the 1992 General Election (Virginia Bottomley and Gillian Shephard). Mr Blair appointed five women to his first Cabinet in 1997.

Functions

The Committee on the Machinery of Government (the Haldane Committee) in its report of 1918 attempted to summarise the functions of the Cabinet as follows:

- the final determination of policy to be submitted to Parliament;
- the supreme control of the national executive in accordance with the policy prescribed by Parliament; and
- the continuous co-ordination and delimitation of the activities of the departments of state.

However, the Haldane Committee's view is closer to the 19th century than to modern times. The 19th-century Cabinet was smaller, government involvement in large areas of citizens' lives was less, and there was more time to discuss long-term policy. Today, some decisions are taken by the Prime Minister alone, some in consultation with senior colleagues, others by Cabinet committees, and some by permanent officials. Furthermore, today's policy is not "prescribed by Parliament". Parliament is informed or consulted, asked to pass legislation and approve expenditure; it rarely, if ever, prescribes policy. Other changes since Haldane's time include:

- the greatly increased scope and complexity of the functions of government;

- considerable increase in the power of the Prime Minister;
- increased power and responsibilities of the civil service and the associated agencies; and
- tightening of the party system.

Cabinet meetings

The Cabinet meets once or twice weekly when Parliament is in session, generally on Tuesday mornings. The duration of meetings varies according to the wishes of the Prime Minister: Tony Blair's were said to last no longer than 40 minutes and this practice continues under Gordon Brown. The following rules generally apply to the Cabinet:

- since time is short, there is little opportunity for proper discussion of policy;
- votes are rarely taken;
- the emphasis is on processing the business of government;
- a matter will not be decided in Cabinet if it can be dealt with by the individual Minister or a Cabinet committee;
- memoranda to be discussed must be circulated 48 hours in advance;
- the organisation of Cabinet business is carried out through the Cabinet Secretariat in the Cabinet Office;
- the Cabinet acts as a sort of clearing house for the Government and is the central point of a complex decision-making structure.

Collective responsibility

The doctrine of collective responsibility evolved gradually, as the Cabinet itself developed its constitutional role. In 1878, Lord Salisbury said: "... for all that passes in Cabinet every member who does not resign is absolutely and irretrievably responsible ...". Thus, so long as a person serves as a Minister, he shares in the collective responsibility of all Ministers and must not publicly criticise or dissociate himself from government policy.

The convention has occasionally been suspended. In 1975 there was no attempt to conceal the differences of opinion within the Cabinet on the question of remaining within the European Community. Ministers who disagreed with the majority view (that continued membership of the EEC should be recommended to the electorate) were free to speak and campaign on the issue outside Parliament. Furthermore, on certain issues of conscience (for example, capital punishment, abortion or euthanasia) a free vote is universally accepted. The doctrine of collective responsibility has a number of political advantages:

- it reinforces party unity;
- it helps to maintain the Government's control over legislation and public expenditure;
- it veils disagreements between departments;
- it reinforces the traditional secrecy which pervades the decision-making process; and
- it helps to maintain the authority of the Prime Minister.

Cabinet Committees

The 19th-century Cabinet set up ad hoc committees to consider particular problems (such as the conduct of the Crimean War), and to draft legislation, among other things. The first permanent committee was set up in 1903: the Committee of Imperial Defence. This showed the value of a permanent committee charged with a major policy area. In both World Wars, a comprehensive system of committees was set up, and after 1945 the Labour Government adopted the system to peace-time use. It has remained ever since.

The committees are intended to consider particular policy areas in detail. They have more time than the Cabinet to do this and the Cabinet usually endorses their recommendations and decisions. Where a committee decision is unanimous, the Cabinet will not normally re-open the issue. The committees' members need not all be Cabinet Ministers, and they are paralleled by committees of officials from relevant departments. The present Government has a large number of Cabinet Committees, including a Constitutional Affairs Committee and a Social Exclusion Committee. For a full list of the current committees, see http://www.pm.gov.uk/output/Page10601.asp

Legislative power

Though the Cabinet is an executive body, it has wide powers over legislation, derived from the position it enjoys as head of the ruling party pledged to carry out a legislative programme based on its manifesto. This programme tends to crowd out most other legislation. A large proportion of parliamentary time is spent in considering and passing Government Bills. Special importance thus attaches to the Legislative Programme Committee of the Cabinet, which has the remit of dealing with the complex Government legislative programme, chaired by the Leader of the House of Commons and the Lord Privy Seal.

MINISTERS OF THE CROWN AND CENTRAL GOVERNMENT DEPARTMENTS

The increase in state intervention in the economy and aspects of social policy in the 19th and 20th centuries gave rise to a considerable growth in the structure and functions of central government. Initially, the administration of such functions was delegated to ad hoc bodies unaccountable to Parliament. Following demands for accountability, such functions were largely transferred, during the latter part of the 19th century, to existing or newly created government departments each under the control of a Minister of the Crown who was directly responsible to Parliament. It is principally through such departments that government policy is put into effect after Parliament has enacted legislation.

Ministers and Secretaries of State

The Sovereign, on the advice of the Prime Minister, appoints Ministers. Some offices (for example, Lord Chancellor, or Secretary of State) derive their existence from the Royal Prerogative, but statutory functions can be assigned to them. The Minister is created a corporation sole, given a seal of office and entrusted with a loosely defined range of functions known as a portfolio. The major departments of state are usually headed by a Secretary of State (for example, the Secretary of State for Defence) and particular prestige has always attached to this office. As a matter of strict law, a Secretary's duties are interchangeable, but in practice are limited to those related to the department in question and some powers and duties may be conferred on a specific Secretary of State by statute or Order in Council. There were 17 designated Secretaries of State as of May 2007.

In addition to Secretaries of State and other Cabinet Ministers, some of whom do not have departmental responsibilities, for example the Lord Privy Seal, there are Ministers of State with particular responsibilities for part of a department's work, and Parliamentary Under-Secretaries of State.

The number of Ministers who may be paid, sit and vote in the House of Commons at any one time is limited to 95 by s 2(1) of the House of Commons Disqualification Act 1975. The purpose of this provision is to limit the powers of patronage of the Prime Minister, but there is no legal limit on the number of Ministers who can be appointed. Thus, some holders of Ministerial office are not in the House of Commons, but in the House of Lords.

By convention, Ministers should be members of one or other House to ensure contact with the legislature, and reinforce the doctrine of ministerial responsibility – but this is not a rule of law. They are almost always political appointments, although the Law Officers of the Crown may be appointed on a non-political basis. The Law Officers of the UK Government are the Attorney-General, the Advocate-General for Scotland and the Solicitor-General. Now that the Scottish Parliament is operational, the Lord Advocate and the Solicitor-General for Scotland are part of the Scottish Executive (Scotland Act 1998, s 48).

The Deputy Prime Minister/First Secretary of State

The post of Deputy Prime Minister has been used infrequently, and its status and functions are at the whim of the Prime Minister of the day. The post has traditionally been coupled with some other Cabinet post, such as First Secretary of State. It has become customary for Labour Governments to include a Deputy Prime Minister to reflect the status of the Deputy Leader of the Labour Party. However, a Conservative Prime Minister may personally choose whether or not to appoint such a Deputy.

Powers and duties of Ministers

The majority of Ministers' powers are derived from statute. Generally, powers are conferred on Ministers, not on departments, and, legally speaking, all decisions taken in departments are those of the Minister. But in practice a great deal of decision-making is carried out by officials, given the vast amount of work which has to be dealt with at any one time. Normally, this is unproblematic since many decisions are fairly routine. Sometimes, however, there are concerns that a Minister is not in control of his department and that civil servants have too much control over policy.

Financial interests

A Minister must not allow a conflict to arise between his public responsibilities and private interests. Detailed rules have been laid down in the *Ministerial Code: A Code of Ethics and Procedural Guidance* for Ministers. Ministers must not, among other things:

- be directors of public companies;
- hold shareholdings which could cause a conflict of interest; or
- use inside information obtained in government for financial gain.

There are also quite detailed rules about the acceptance of gifts, hospitality or services which would, or might appear to, place the Minister under an obligation.

Ministerial responsibility

The doctrine of ministerial responsibility performs the function of securing a level of accountability and control over the executive by Parliament. There are two aspects of responsibility: collective and individual. Under the doctrine of collective ministerial responsibility, all Ministers must either accept Cabinet decisions or dissent publicly and resign, unless collective responsibility is waived by the Cabinet on a particular issue. This mechanism allows Governments to show a united front to Parliament and the public. Collective responsibility is followed slavishly by Governments since the executive must be seen as strong and there can be no doubt over its policies. Thus, if a Minister is placed under parliamentary pressure on a particular issue, the remainder of the Government will rally to give support since the policy will be a common one.

On the other hand, individual ministerial responsibility ensures that Ministers are responsible to Parliament for the administration of their individual departments, ie a Minister is accountable for not only personal decisions but also the actions and decisions of civil servants. The most infamous example of this doctrine can be found in the Crichel Down Affair when the Air Ministry had compulsorily purchased land for defence purposes in 1938. By 1954, the land was no longer required and it was transferred to the Ministry of Agriculture which ultimately let it out to a tenant. The original owner of the land was neither consulted nor offered the opportunity to regain ownership. An inquiry into the affair discovered that many other landowners had been similarly affected and that the Ministry had acted in an underhand fashion. This resulted in widespread parliamentary and public condemnation and the Minister for Agriculture, Thomas Dugdale, resigned, taking full responsibility for the actions of his department. Similarly, in 1982, the Foreign Secretary, Lord Carrington, took personal responsibility for mismanagement of the Foreign and Commonwealth Office in failing to appreciate the threat of Argentine invasion of the Falklands.

In most cases, attempts are made to invoke ministerial responsibility by parliamentary questions or debate. In this way, parliamentary criticism can lead to public condemnation and might cause a resignation, but such resignations are becoming increasingly rare. In modern times, there has been a blurring of the distinction between questions of mismanagement and personal behaviour and many resignations since 1945 have in fact involved questions of personal conduct, such as those of John Profumo in 1963 (who lied to the House) and David Mellor in 1992 who was eventually forced out of the Cabinet following a war of attrition with the newspapers over his moral conduct. More recently, the former Home Secretary, David Blunkett, was forced to resign after his private life led to the alleged speeding-up of an immigration application for the nanny of his son.

In recent years, given the growth in the number of executive Next Steps Agencies, the notion of ministerial responsibility has been identified with the idea of ministerial accountability, and a policy/operational dichotomy has developed in some government departments. Thus, the blame for many acts of mismanagement within a government department may be attached to the agency head or civil servant directorate involved instead of, or as well as, the Minister. Corrective action within the department will, however, be undertaken by the Minister.

Organisation of central departments

Government departments have the responsibility of carrying out the core functions of government in the UK. They initiate the vast majority of Government legislation and have powers and functions laid out by statute, subject to some ministerial powers which are exercised by virtue of the Royal Prerogative. Departments have a clear structure and are headed by a Minister or Secretary of State who is assisted by civil servants in the formulation of policy and legislation. The doctrine of ministerial responsibility ensures that Ministers are ultimately accountable to Parliament for the actions of their departments and officials.

The Ministers of the Crown Act 1975 allows for departments to be re-structured and responsibilities to be transferred through Order in Council. These powers have been utilised on a number of occasions in order to reflect ever-changing policy objectives within the Government. The degree of discretion available to government departments can be considerable and, besides ministerial responsibility, they are also subject to scrutiny by the Parliamentary Commissioner for Administration concerning instances of maladministration.

Non-departmental public bodies

Non-departmental bodies (NDPBs) can be found in various forms and include the National Health Service, public corporations such as the BBC, and Next Steps Agencies. An important development in the organisation of governmental functions can be seen in the creation of Next Steps Agencies. They have responsibility for the execution of policy on a day-to-day basis and high levels of responsibility are delegated to Agency managers. Their powers are set down in framework agreements made between the relevant department and the Agency concerned. The agreement will outline present and future objectives for the Agency, financial arrangements, personnel and staffing policy, and review procedures. The head of a Next Steps Agency is the Chief Executive, who is appointed on a contract of employment limited to around 5 years in duration.

The exact position of Next Steps Agencies is uncertain and one of the criticisms of their growing use is the perceived lack of accountability to Parliament. The Government, however, is assured that accountability is achieved through Agency Chief Executives being accountable to the relevant Minister who, in turn, is accountable to Parliament. Their work is also scrutinised by Select Committees and the Public Accounts Committee.

In addition, there are a number of other quasi-autonomous non-governmental bodies known as "quangos". Such bodies are invariably created by statute and well-known examples include the Scottish Development Agency, the Equal Opportunities Commission and the Civil Aviation Authority. As creatures of statute, quangos must keep within their statutory powers, and may be controlled by the courts if they act outside their statutory powers. Ministers may also issue directions or guidelines regulating the behaviour of the body. Quangos are often criticised as being unelected and unaccountable since they are outside the scope of mainstream political control and their members are appointed by the Government.

Essential Facts

- The Government of the UK consists of the monarch, the Prime Minister, the Cabinet and other Ministers of the Crown.
- The Prime Minister is appointed by the Queen and is normally the leader of the party which has won the largest number of seats in a General Election.
- The Prime Minister is the most powerful member of the Government and, by convention, is a Member of the House of Commons.
- The Cabinet is the name given to a special committee of senior Ministers who are responsible for making and controlling government policy.
- The Cabinet reflects the collective leadership of the majority party in the House of Commons and, through its control of that party, the Cabinet exercises control over Parliament.

- Ministerial responsibility ensures that Ministers are responsible to Parliament for the administration of their individual departments, ie a Minister is accountable for not only personal decisions but also the actions and decisions of civil servants.
- In most cases, attempts are made to invoke ministerial responsibility by parliamentary questions or debate. In this way, parliamentary criticism can lead to public condemnation and may cause a resignation, but such resignations are becoming increasingly rare.

8 THE SCOTTISH PARLIAMENT

Until 1707, Scotland had its own Parliament, quite separate from that of England. For various reasons, mainly economic, the union of the two Parliaments was proposed in the early years of the 18th century and in 1707 the Parliament of England and the Parliament of Scotland passed separate Acts of Union. As a result, these Parliaments ceased to exist and were replaced by the Parliament of the United Kingdom of Great Britain. The union was not popular with many of the Scottish people. In fact, there was rioting in the streets of Glasgow and Edinburgh when the terms were made public. However, because of Scotland's poor economic state, the union was almost inevitable and it was largely tolerated for over 150 years.

A number of factors, including the rise of the Irish Home Rule movement in the 19th century, led to the emergence of a Scottish Home Rule Association in 1886. The National Party for Scotland was founded in 1928 and began to contest elections. Six years later, it merged with another party, the Scottish Party, to form the Scottish National Party (SNP). It was not until the late 1960s and early 1970s that the SNP began to make real headway in terms of winning seats in the UK Parliament and in Scottish Councils. The Welsh nationalist party, Plaid Cymru, was also having some electoral success.

The Labour Government elected in 1974 lacked an outright majority and was forced to make concessions to the nationalists. Eventually in 1977, directly elected assemblies for Scotland and Wales were proposed in separate Scotland and Wales Bills. During the parliamentary process an amendment was introduced which made it necessary for 40 per cent of the electorates to vote "Yes" in referenda before the Acts could be brought into operation. The 40 per cent threshold was not met either in Scotland or in Wales, although, in the case of the Scotland Act 1978, the majority of those who voted did vote "Yes". This led to a vote of no confidence in the Labour Government which was passed and the Government fell. The Conservatives won the ensuing General Election in May 1979 and repealed the Scotland and Wales Acts 1978 almost immediately.

The Conservative Government remained implacably opposed to devolution during its 18 years in power but the desire for some form of devolution remained in Scotland. A Campaign for a Scottish Assembly was set up in 1980, from which grew a cross-party Scottish Constitutional Convention (SCC). This Convention published a number of documents advocating a Scottish Parliament.

The Labour and Liberal Democrat Parties included a commitment to a Scottish Parliament, based on the SCC's proposals, in their manifestos for the 1997 election. The Labour Party won that election and within 3 months produced a White Paper which set out plans for a devolved Parliament with legislative and limited tax-varying powers. These plans were endorsed in a referendum of the Scottish people and the Scotland Act was passed in 1998. The first General Election to the Scottish Parliament was held in May 1999 and on 1 July the Parliament was formally opened by the Queen and assumed its full powers.

THE POWERS OF THE SCOTTISH PARLIAMENT

The powers of the Scottish Parliament are not listed in the Scotland Act 1998. Instead, there are lists of the powers which the UK Parliament decided not to devolve to the Scottish Parliament. These are said to be reserved to the UK Parliament. Any power which is not listed is assumed to be devolved to the Scottish Parliament and within its legislative competence. This means that the Scottish Parliament has the power to make law in these areas. However, because the UK Parliament remains the supreme law-making body for the UK, that Parliament retains the power to make laws for Scotland in the devolved areas.

Matters reserved to the UK Parliament

The reserved matters are listed in Sch 5 to the Scotland Act 1998. There are general reservations and specific reservations.

General reservations include:

- the Crown;
- the Union of Scotland and England;
- the UK Parliament;
- the continued existence of the Scottish High Courts;
- most aspects of foreign affairs;
- the defence of the realm;
- the armed forces;
- the registration and funding of political parties;
- the civil service;
- treason.

Specific reservations are too detailed to list here in their entirety. They are grouped under 11 heads and include:

- financial and economic matters;
- many aspects of home affairs;
- trade and industry;
- energy;
- many aspects of transport;
- social security;
- regulation of the professions;
- employment rights and duties and industrial relations;
- medicine and some aspects of health;
- regulatory responsibilities relating to TV and radio broadcasting and some minor matters relating to libraries;
- miscellaneous matters including most aspects of equal opportunities; weapons of mass destruction; time scales and zones; and the regulation of activities in outer space.

From an examination of the lists of reserved matters, we can deduce the matters devolved to the Scottish Parliament. Broadly speaking, these include:

- overall responsibility for the NHS in Scotland;
- education and training;
- local government; social work; housing; and land use planning;
- many aspects of economic development, including tourism;
- many aspects of transport;
- most aspects of civil and criminal law; the criminal justice system; courts and tribunals; prisons;
- police and fire services; civil defence; and emergency planning;
- protection of animals;
- environmental protection; water and sewerage; flood prevention; and the natural and built heritages;
- agriculture; forestry and fishing; and food standards;
- sport and the arts;
- miscellaneous matters including statistics, public records and registers.

The Scottish Parliament also has the power, within limits, to amend or repeal Acts of the UK Parliament which relate to devolved matters. The Human Rights Act 1998 is completely protected from modification, as are most aspects of the Scotland Act 1998 itself and the European Communities Act 1972.

FINANCING THE SCOTTISH PARLIAMENT

The main source of finance for the Scottish Parliament and the Scottish Executive is a block grant allocated by the UK Government and Parliament. The level of the block grant is decided from year to year, in accordance with a formula which decides the level of spending between Scotland, England and Wales. This is known as the "Barnett formula", after the Chief Secretary to the Treasury in 1978 when the formula was devised.

The Scottish Parliament also has the power to increase or decrease the basic rate of income tax for Scottish taxpayers by up to 3 pence in the pound. This power has not yet been utilised by the Parliament.

MEMBERS OF THE SCOTTISH PARLIAMENT AND ELECTIONS

There are 129 Members of the Scottish Parliament, commonly known as MSPs. They are elected by a form of proportional representation known as the Additional Member System. Of these, 73 are constituency members, elected by the traditional method of "first past the post". The remaining 56 are regional members. They are allocated seats on the basis of a second vote cast not for an individual but for a political party. This "tops up" the political parties' representation and enables minority parties to be represented in the Scottish Parliament. It is also possible for people without any political affiliation to stand as independents. Both the constituency and the regional MSPs have the same status in law.

Ordinary General Elections to the Scottish Parliament are normally held on the first Thursday of May every four years. The first of these was held on 6 May 1999. An extraordinary General Election may be held in two situations. The first of these is when at least two-thirds of the MSPs vote for an earlier election. This might be because the Parliament had become unworkable because of deadlock between the political parties. This has not yet happened in the life of the Parliament. The second situation is where, for some reason such as the death or resignation of the incumbent, the office of First Minister has been vacant for a period of 28 days.

If the seat of a constituency member falls vacant, a by-election will be held, normally within 3 months, to elect a replacement. If the seat of a regional member who was elected from a political party list falls vacant, the vacancy is filled by the person next on that party's list who is willing to serve and is acceptable to the party concerned. If the regional seat had been held by an independent, the seat remains vacant until the next General Election.

The right to vote in Scottish parliamentary elections is based on similar principles to the right to vote in UK parliamentary elections but is extended to include members of the House of Lords and European Union citizens resident in Scotland.

To stand for election to the Scottish Parliament, a person must be 21 and a British, Commonwealth, Irish or European citizen resident in the UK. Several categories of people are disqualified from standing for election to the Scottish Parliament, as follows:

- judges;
- civil servants, including the staff of the Scottish Executive;
- members of the armed forces;
- members of police forces;
- members of foreign legislatures;
- holders of certain public offices;
- senior local government officers who hold politically restricted posts;
- undischarged bankrupts;
- persons suffering from mental illness;
- convicted prisoners serving a sentence of more than 1 year;
- persons convicted of corrupt or illegal electoral practices.

There are no provisions in the Scotland Act 1998 to ensure that an equal number of male and female MSPs are elected. However, in the selection of candidates for the first General Election in 1999, the Labour Party "twinned" constituencies in most of Scotland and instructed their members to select one man and one woman for each pair of seats. This resulted in 28 men and 28 women being elected as Labour MSPs. In addition 20 more women from other parties were elected. The number of women MSPs rose to 51 (35.9 per cent) after the election in 2003. This is one of the highest percentages of female representation in parliaments throughout the world. It stayed roughly the same in 2007.

There is nothing in the Scotland Act 1998 to prevent dual mandates. Having a dual mandate means that an individual is an elected member of two bodies and thus has a mandate from two sets of electors. Thus, it is possible for someone who is a member of the UK or European Parliaments or a local councillor to be elected as an MSP.

HOW THE SCOTTISH PARLIAMENT WORKS

Most parliaments in the world meet both in plenary session (ie with all members entitled to be present) and in committees where more detailed work is done by a smaller number of members. The Scottish Parliament is no different. The working week lasts from Monday afternoon till Friday lunchtime. This allows MSPs to travel from their constituencies and regions on a Monday morning and return on a Friday afternoon. The Parliament meets in plenary session normally on Wednesday afternoon and all day Thursday and is chaired by the Presiding Officer. The various committees meet when the Parliament is not in plenary session.

The committees have been described as the "power house" of the Parliament. The two main types of committee are mandatory committees, which the Parliament *must* establish, and subject committees, which the Parliament *may* establish. The eight mandatory committees include the Finance and Audit Committees, the Standards Committee, which deals with MSPs' conduct, and the Public Petitions Committee. Subject committees include the Education Committee and the Rural Affairs Committee. For an up-to-date list of committees, see http://www. scottish.parliament.uk/business/committees/index.htm

Plenary sessions

The Scotish Parliament meets in plenary session for various purposes. The main ones are:

- some of the stages in the law-making process (see below);
- First Minister's Question Time, where the First Minister answers questions put down mainly by members of the Opposition parties;
- Question Time, when other Scottish Ministers answer questions put down by MSPs generally;
- to receive general statements of policy made by the Scottish Ministers;
- debates on general policy issues;
- debates on motions of no confidence in the Scottish Executive or an individual Minister;
- to hear distinguished visitors.

Committee sessions

The committees are used mainly for the following purposes:

- some of the stages in the law-making process (see below);

- to examine any matter within its remit referred to it by the Parliament or another committee;
- to consider the policy and administration of the Scottish Executive on any matter within its remit;
- to examine any matters within its remit which it considers appropriate;
- to consider the need for reform of the law in areas within the committee's remit;
- to initiate Bills on any matter within its remit;
- to consider financial proposals and the financial administration by the Scottish Executive of matters within the committee's remit.

Committees normally meet in public, not necessarily in Edinburgh, and can take evidence from experts and members of the public in considering any of the above.

MAKING LAW

Making law is probably the most important function of any parliament. The Scotland Act 1998 gives the Scottish Parliament the power to make laws but this power is limited to matters which have not been reserved to the UK Parliament. In addition, the Scottish Parliament cannot make a valid law which is incompatible with the Human Rights Act 1998 or with European Community law. Detailed provisions are built into the Scotland Act to ensure that each proposal for legislation (known as a Bill) is subjected to scrutiny to prevent any provision creeping in which is outside the powers of the Scottish Parliament.

When a Bill is introduced into the Parliament, the Presiding Officer must provide a written statement indicating whether or not, in his view, the provisions of the Bill are within the legislative competence of the Scottish Parliament. If the Bill is an Executive Bill, the member of the Scottish Executive in charge of it should provide a similar written statement.

In addition, when a Bill has been passed by the Parliament, certain Law Officers of the Scottish Parliament and the UK Parliament may refer the Bill to the Judicial Committee of the Privy Council for a decision as to its legislative competence. This reference must be made within 4 weeks of the Bill being passed by the Parliament. Secretaries of State in the UK Government may also intervene, again within 4 weeks of the passing of the Bill, primarily if they believe that any provision of the Bill is incompatible with the UK's international obligations or the interests of defence or national security. They do this by making an order prohibiting the Presiding Officer from submitting the Bill for Royal Assent.

The stages of a Bill

A Bill normally passes through three stages and is then presented for Royal Assent when it becomes an Act of the Scottish Parliament known as an "asp". There are three main types of Bill:

- Executive Bills, which are the most common, introduced by a member of the Scottish Executive;
- Committee Bills, introduced by one of the Parliament's Committees; and
- Members' Bills, introduced by an MSP who is not a member of the Scottish Executive.

The Scottish Parliament may also pass Private Bills, which are mainly sponsored by local authorities.

Consultation

As the Scottish Parliament has no second chamber, such as the House of Lords in the UK Parliament, to act as a revising chamber, care has to be taken before a Bill starts on its progress to ensure that ambiguities and anomalies are removed as far as possible. So, best practice is for consultation with interested parties, expert bodies and the like to be carried out before the Bill is introduced into the Parliament.

Accompanying documents

In addition to the Presiding Officer's and, in appropriate cases, Scottish Executive member's written statements as to the legislative competence of the Bill, there is a requirement for certain other accompanying documents. These are:

- a financial memorandum setting out an estimate of the costs to which the provisions of the Bill might give rise;
- explanatory notes summarising the provisions of the Bill;
- a policy memorandum which sets out the policy objectives of the Bill, details of any consultation carried out and an assessment of any impact on equal opportunities, human rights, island communities, local government and sustainable development.

Stage 1

Once a Bill has been introduced and printed, it is referred to the committee of the Parliament within whose remit the subject-matter falls.

This committee is known as the "lead committee". The lead committee considers the general principles of the Bill and prepares a report for the Parliament, taking account of any evidence submitted by interested groups and individuals. The Parliament in plenary session then considers the general principles of the Bill in the light of the lead committee's report and votes on whether these principles are agreed to. If so, the Bill is referred back, normally to the lead committee, for Stage 2. At least 7 sitting days must elapse before this stage can start.

Stage 2

The lead committee examines the Bill section by section and considers amendments. Each section must be agreed to by the committee. At least 9 sitting days must elapse if the Bill is amended at Stage 2, or 4 days if it is unamended, before the Bill proceeds to Stage 3.

Stage 3

Stage 3 is taken by the Parliament in plenary session and the Parliament must decide whether to pass the Bill or not, or to refer it back to the lead committee for further Stage 2 consideration. If there is a vote on whether the Bill is to be passed or not, more than a quarter of the MSPs must take part in the vote, ie at least 33.

Reconsideration stage

This will only take place if one of the Law Officers or a Secretary of State has intervened (see above). The reconsideration stage is taken by the Parliament in plenary session and only amendments which would resolve the problem raised by the Law Officer or the Secretary of State can be made. Once the amendments have been disposed of, the Parliament must decide whether to approve the Bill.

The procedures for passing Committee Bills and Members' Bills are very similar to those described above. In the case of a Member's Bill, the MSP proposing the Bill must gather the support of at least 11 other MSPs, within 1 month of publishing the proposal. Otherwise, the proposal falls.

The procedures for a Private Bill are more complicated and involve the establishment of a Private Bill Committee which must give the promoter of the Bill and any objectors the opportunity to present evidence to the members.

The Scottish Parliament passes around 16 Acts each session, the majority of which are Executive Bills. However, the opportunities for non-Executive members of the Scottish Parliament successfully to promote Members' Bills are better than those for Members of the UK Parliament. Committee Bills have no equivalent in the UK Parliament. It should be noted that Scottish Ministers have the power to make law, called subordinate legislation, in the form of Scottish Statutory Instruments (SSIs).

THE SCOTTISH PARLIAMENT AND THE COURTS

The Scottish Parliament is a creation of the UK Parliament and is not a sovereign body. This means that its Acts may be successfully challenged in the courts as being *ultra vires* (or beyond the powers of) the Scottish Parliament. Similarly, actions of the Scottish Executive can be challenged as being beyond the authority granted to the Executive by the Scotland Act 1998. These challenges are called "devolution issues" and can arise in virtually any court or tribunal, in civil or criminal cases.

Most of the cases in which devolution issues have been raised so far have been criminal cases where it has been alleged that the Lord Advocate has brought a prosecution which is in some way incompatible with the European Convention on Human Rights. One such case which had significant repercussions is *Starrs* v *Ruxton* (2000). Starrs was being tried before one of the temporary sheriffs appointed by the Lord Advocate on year-long contracts. Article 6(1) of the ECHR guarantees "a fair and public hearing ... before an independent and impartial tribunal established by law". It was successfully argued for Starrs that a temporary sheriff on a short-term contract might not be independent and impartial as he could be influenced in his decision-making by the desire to avoid unpopularity with the Lord Advocate. The decision in this case led to the removal of temporary sheriffs from the Bench in Scotland.

A few cases have involved challenges to the validity of provisions of Acts of the Scottish Parliament. An early case concerned the very first Act passed by the Scottish Parliament. This was *Anderson* v *Scottish Ministers* (2003). After Anderson was convicted of culpable homicide, he was kept under a restriction order in the State Mental Hospital under the Mental Health (Public Safety and Appeals) (Scotland) Act 1999. He argued that s 1 of the 1999 Act was incompatible with Art 5 of the ECHR (which concerns the right to liberty) and was therefore outside the legislative competence of the Scottish Parliament. However, the Privy Council, which is the highest court of appeal in devolution issues, held that the 1999 Act was not incompatible with Art 5 of the ECHR as it contains exceptions which allow for the detention of people of unsound mind.

Another example can be found in *Adams and Others* v *Scottish Ministers* (2004). The Act which was being challenged was the Protection of Wild Mammals (Scotland) Act 2002 which made fox hunting with dogs illegal. Adams was a manager of foxhounds. He, along with others who participated in fox hunting, argued that the ban on fox hunting breached Art 8 of the ECHR (respect for private and family life) and Art 11 (right to freedom of peaceful assembly and association with others). If these were breaches then provisions of the Act were outside the legislative competence of the Scottish Parliament and therefore invalid. The court was not convinced of these arguments and held that the Act was valid.

So far, there has not been a successful challenge to the validity of an Act of the Scottish Parliament.

PUBLIC PARTICIPATION

Meaningful participation by the people of Scotland in the work of the Scottish Parliament was seen by its founders as a key element in the operation of the Parliament. The Parliament and its committees almost always meet in public and there is a fairly large public gallery. Consultation on Bill proposals also allows for participation by members of the public.

In particular, to enable members of the public to bring issues to the attention of the Parliament, a Public Petitions Committee has been established as a mandatory committee. The members decide whether a petition is admissible and, if so, can refer the petition to the Scottish Ministers or to the appropriate committee for them to take appropriate action. The Committee has considered hundreds of petitions, covering a wide range of topics including housing, transport, the protection of heritage sites, genetically modified crops and many others.

Proceedings of the Parliament and its committees are reported in the Scottish Parliament Official Report and there are also arrangements for broadcasting proceedings. The Scottish Parliament also has a website where current information may be obtained. See http://www.scottish.parliament.uk/home.htm.

Essential Facts

- The Scottish Parliament was established in 1999, by the Scotland Act 1998.

- The Scottish Parliament is elected by the form of proportional representation known as the Additional Member System.
- The rules relating to the rights to vote and to stand for election to the Scottish Parliament are similar to those for the UK Parliament but include members of the House of Lords and EU citizens resident in Scotland.
- The UK Parliament has devolved certain law-making powers to the Scottish Parliament, but the Scottish Parliament cannot make law in the areas which the UK Parliament has reserved to itself.
- The Scottish Parliament has the power to increase or decrease the basic rate of income tax paid by Scottish taxpayers by a maximum of 3 pence in the pound.
- The role of committees in the Scottish Parliament is more significant than the role of committees in the UK Parliament.

Essential Cases

Starrs v Ruxton (2000): this concerned the removal of temporary sheriffs from the Bench in Scotland. Article 6(1) of the ECHR guarantees "a fair and public hearing ... before an independent and impartial tribunal established by law". A temporary sheriff on a short-term contract was not independent or impartial, as he could be influenced in his decision-making by the desire to avoid unpopularity with the Lord Advocate.

Anderson v Scottish Ministers (2003): an unsuccessful challenge to the compatibility of s 1 of the Mental Health (Public Safety and Appeals) (Scotland) Act 1999 with Art 5 ECHR (concerning the right to liberty) and that it was therefore outside the legislative competence of the Scottish Parliament.

Adams and Others v Scottish Ministers (2004): an unsuccessful challenge that the Protection of Wild Mammals (Scotland) Act 2002 breached Art 8 ECHR (respect for private and family life) and Art 11 (right to freedom of peaceful assembly and association with others) and was therefore outside the legislative competence of the Scottish Parliament.

9 THE SCOTTISH EXECUTIVE

The establishment of the Scottish Parliament has given Scotland not only a legislature, but also a Government which can take executive action over the whole range of devolved functions. The Scotland Act 1998 describes it as the "Scottish Administration" but it is generally known as the "Scottish Executive" and sometimes as the "Scottish Government". Rather confusingly, the term "Scottish Executive" is also used to describe the civil servants who support the Scottish Government.

When the term is used of the Scottish Government, the Scottish Executive consists of the First Minister, the Scottish Ministers and the Scottish Law Officers. The rules for the appointment of the First Minister and the other Scottish Ministers are to be found in the Scotland Act 1998. This is in sharp contrast to the rules for the appointment of the Prime Minister and the Ministers in the UK Government which are unwritten and based on convention.

THE FIRST MINISTER

The First Minister is the equivalent of the Prime Minister in the Scottish Parliament. He is appointed by the Queen from among the MSPs within 28 days of a General Election and holds office "during Her Majesty's pleasure". Theoretically, this means that the First Minister could be dismissed by the Queen for good reason or for none. In practice, the First Minister holds office for as long as he can command the support of a majority of the MSPs. Therefore the person appointed as First Minister is normally the leader of the party which has won the largest number of seats. Since the electoral system of the Scottish Parliament has an element of proportional representation in it, it is unlikely that any one party will win a clear majority of seats.

The 28-day period referred to above is to allow the party leaders time to attempt to form a coalition government (or opt for a minority government) and decide on a First Minister. Failure to do so within the 28 days would lead to another General Election, which would be unpopular with the electorate, and this time limit therefore puts pressure on the various parties to come to an agreement as to which party or parties should form the Government.

In the elections of 1999 and 2003, the Labour Party won the largest number of seats, but not a clear majority, and on each occasion a coalition was formed between the Labour and Liberal Democrat Parties. In May 2007, the Scottish National Party won 47 of the 129 seats and the Labour Party won 46. None of the other parties was prepared to enter into a coalition agreement with either of these parties and the SNP, as the largest party, decided to form a minority government. The Scottish Parliament agreed to appoint Alex Salmond, their leader, as First Minister. This took place 14 days after the election.

The person who is to be First Minister has to be nominated by an MSP, in writing to the Presiding Officer and the nomination seconded by another MSP. If there is more than one candidate, there is a vote or series of votes until one single candidate emerges who has the support of the majority of MSPs voting. The Presiding Officer recommends the successful candidate to the Queen and the Queen appoints the candidate.

If the office of First Minister falls vacant, a new First Minister must be nominated for appointment within 28 days of the post falling vacant, otherwise an extraordinary General Election must be held.

SCOTTISH MINISTERS

The First Minister appoints a team of Scottish Ministers from among the Members of the Scottish Parliament. The Scottish Ministers are appointed with the Queen's approval but the First Minister must obtain the agreement of the Scottish Parliament to the nominations before submitting names to the Queen. This is different from the procedure at Westminster, where the Prime Minister can recommend to the Queen the appointment of whomsoever he wishes to ministerial office, subject, of course, to political considerations, without having to secure the agreement of Parliament.

The MSPs can reject, but not substitute, the names of particular individuals in the First Minister's list. The allocation of portfolios to Ministers is a decision for the First Minister alone, subject to negotiation with the coalition partners (if any). The Scottish Ministers, like the First Minister, hold office at Her Majesty's pleasure. They may be removed from office by the First Minister and must resign if they lose the confidence of the Parliament.

In addition to the oath of allegiance to the Queen which all members of the Scottish Parliament must take on election, members of the Scottish Executive must take another oath, as follows: "I swear that I will well and truly serve Her Majesty Queen Elizabeth in the office of Scottish Minister". The number of Ministers appointed to the Scottish Executive was about 10 under the Labour/Liberal Democrat coalitions of 1999 and 2003, compared with the 20 or so Ministers appointed to the UK Cabinet.

However, the First Minister of the SNP minority Government of 2007 appointed only five Ministers to the Cabinet and re-named them "Cabinet Secretaries".

JUNIOR SCOTTISH MINISTERS

The First Minister may also appoint Junior Scottish Ministers. Technically, they are not members of the Scottish Executive as defined in the Scotland Act 1998, although they are generally considered as such. They are appointed in the same way as Scottish Ministers. With the agreement of the Parliament, the First Minister recommends their appointment to the Queen. They too hold office at Her Majesty's pleasure, may be removed from office by the First Minister, may resign at any time and must do so if the Scottish Executive loses the confidence of the Scottish Parliament. Their salaries as well as their rank are below those of full Scottish Ministers. The number of Junior Scottish Ministers appointed in May 2007 was 10.

THE SCOTTISH LAW OFFICERS

There are two Scottish Law Officers, namely the Lord Advocate (and his deputy) and the Solicitor General, both of whom act as the senior legal advisers to the Scottish Executive. They, too, are members of the Scottish Government. In other words, they are political appointments. The Lord Advocate is also the head of the system of criminal prosecution and investigation of deaths in Scotland and must act independently in those capacities.

Unlike the other Scottish Ministers, the Scottish Law Officers do not have to be Members of the Scottish Parliament and none of the Lords Advocate or Solicitors General, since the inception of the Scottish Parliament in 1999, have been elected members of the Scottish Parliament. In fact, they may not even be members of any political party, let alone the one(s) forming the Scottish Executive. The reason for this is that they must be legally qualified and it may not be possible to find two MSPs who have the appropriate qualifications. They are appointed in the same way as Scottish Ministers are, with the approval of the Scottish Parliament. They can participate in the proceedings of the Parliament and its committees, but cannot vote.

There are several provisions in the Scotland Act 1998 which are designed to protect the independence of the Lord Advocate from interference. For example, it is outwith the competence of the Scottish

Parliament to pass an Act to remove the Lord Advocate from the position as head of the systems of criminal prosecution and investigation of deaths in Scotland. As a member of the Scottish Executive, the Lord Advocate originally had a seat in the Scottish Cabinet. This came in for a certain amount of criticism, on the basis that this could be seen to undermine the independence of the post. As a result of such criticism, in 2000, the Lord Advocate gave up the right to vote in the Cabinet but remained a member of the Scottish Executive.

Following the election in 2007, the newly elected SNP First Minister took the unusual step of re-appointing the Lord Advocate who had been appointed by the previous Labour/Liberal Democrat administration. However, it was decided that she should not be a member of the Cabinet. This further protects the political independence of the post.

MOTIONS OF NO CONFIDENCE

It is a convention of the UK constitution that the Prime Minister and his Ministers must resign if they lose a motion of no confidence passed by Parliament. In the case of the Scottish Parliament, this is now statutory and the Scotland Act 1998 lays out the procedure in some detail. Any MSP may move a motion of no confidence, but must have the support of at least 25 other MSPs. Only a simple majority of those voting is required for the motion to be passed. If a new First Minister is not appointed within 28 days, an extraordinary General Election must be held.

THE CIVIL SERVICE

The Scottish Ministers may appoint such staff as they consider appropriate. These are known as civil servants. However, these civil servants remain part of the UK Home Civil Service. This preserves their career structure in the UK and ensures unified terms and conditions of service.

The head of the Civil Service is called the Permanent Secretary. Until 2007, the officers in the Scottish Executive under the Permanent Secretary were allocated to six major departments, each led by a Head of Department. However, following the election in 2007, the management structure of the Scottish Executive was re-organised. The Heads of Department have been replaced by five Directors-General, covering Economy, Health, Education, Environment and Justice/Communities. There is now a Strategic Board which consists of the Permanent Secretary and the five Directors-General who form the Civil Service "top table" of advisers for Scottish Ministers.

Essential Facts

- When the term is used of the Scottish Government, the "Scottish Executive" consists of the First Minister, the Scottish Ministers and the Scottish Law Officers. Confusingly, the term is also used to describe the civil servants who support the Scottish Government.
- The First Minister is the equivalent of the Prime Minister in the Scottish Parliament. He is appointed by the Queen from among the MSPs within 28 days of a General Election and holds office "during Her Majesty's pleasure".
- The First Minister appoints a team of Scottish Ministers from among the Members of the Scottish Parliament. The Scottish Ministers are appointed with the Queen's approval but the First Minister must obtain the agreement of the Scottish Parliament to the nominations before submitting names to the Queen.
- The First Minister may also appoint Junior Scottish Ministers. Technically, they are not members of the Scottish Executive as defined in the Scotland Act 1998, although they are generally considered as such. They are appointed in the same way as Scottish Ministers.
- There are two Scottish Law Officers, namely the Lord Advocate (and his deputy) and the Solicitor General, both of whom act as the senior legal advisers to the Scottish Executive. They are members of the Scottish Government. The Lord Advocate is also the head of the system of criminal prosecution and investigation of deaths in Scotland and must act independently in those capacities.
- The Scottish Ministers may appoint such staff as they consider appropriate. These are known as civil servants. However, these civil servants remain part of the UK Home Civil Service. This preserves their career structure in the UK and ensures unified terms and conditions of service.

10 JUDICIAL REVIEW

Judicial review refers to the inherent common law power of the Court of Session to review or supervise acts or omissions of administrative bodies. This is known as the supervisory jurisdiction of the Court of Session, and the court has had this power since it was first established in 1532. The supervisory jurisdiction was fully expounded by Lord Shaw in *Moss Empires* v *Assessor for Glasgow* (1917):

> "It is within the jurisdiction of the Court of Session to keep inferior judicatories and administrative bodies right, in the sense of compelling them to keep within the limits of their statutory powers ... but it is not within the power or function of the Court of Session itself to do the work set by the legislator to be performed by those administrative bodies or inferior judicatories themselves."

Thus, the Court of Session has the power to ensure that administrative and other bodies act lawfully. But since Parliament has entrusted the administrative bodies to carry out certain functions, the court cannot intervene just because a *wrong* decision has been made, or one that the court would not have made. The judicial review process is confined to whether the administrative body's decision was wrong in law, not with the *merits* of the decision, as in *Guthrie* v *Miller* (1827), where, under a local Police Act, commissioners of police were entrusted with the discretion to provide lighting in public streets. Guthrie claimed in the Court of Session that the commissioners were failing in their duty. The question at issue was whether a lamp-post was necessary at a particular spot. The court refused to become involved in the question, on the ground that this would involve deciding whether lamp-posts should be on every street corner. That was a question of *fact* to be decided by the local authority and there was no question of *law* to be judicially reviewed by the court.

SCOPE OF JUDICIAL REVIEW

Unlike in England and Wales, judicial review in Scotland does not favour a strict public/private law approach, as is discussed by Lord Hope in the leading decision of *West* v *Secretary of State for Scotland* (1992):

> "The Court of Session has power, in the exercise of its supervisory jurisdiction, to regulate the process by which decisions are taken by any

person or body to whom a jurisdiction, power or authority has been
delegated or entrusted by statute, agreement or any other instrument ...
The competency of the application does not depend upon any distinction
between public law and private law, nor is it confined to those cases which
English law has accepted as amenable to judicial review, nor is it correct
in regard to issues about competency to describe judicial review ... as a
public law remedy."

This is significantly different from the approach taken by the English
courts, where the decision on the competency of a review petition is often
based upon whether the issue has a sufficient public law element (*O'Reilly*
v *Mackman* (1983)). However, in Scotland, review is not confined to the
statutory powers of administrative bodies. It is clear from authority that
the supervisory jurisdiction may also extend to the actions and omissions
of bodies which are clearly "private" in nature: for example, in *McDonald*
v *Burns* (1940), where the Church expelled two nuns from a convent,
and in *St Johnstone FC* v *Scottish Football Association* (1965), where the SFA
fined St Johnstone Football Club. The common characteristic in such
cases is not the nature of the body, but the entrusting to it of a decision-
making power or duty. This was illustrated by Lord Hope in *West*
through the tri-partite relationship which he offers as a useful indicator
for distinguishing reviewable circumstances from those that are purely
contractual obligations.

Diagram 1: Tri-partite relationship

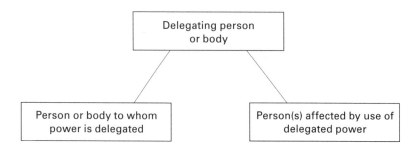

However, Lord Hope's remarks on the tri-partite relationship have
been viewed by some as slightly anomalous. In the cases of *Naik* v *University
of Stirling* (1994) and *Joobeen* v *University of Stirling* (1995), the application
of the tri-partite "test" led to markedly different results even when based

upon identical facts. In both cases, students had been expelled from Stirling University for non-payment of fees, yet in *Naik* the circumstances were held to be reviewable while in *Joobeen* they were not. In *Naik*, Lord MacLean considered that there was a tri-partite relationship since powers to discipline students were granted to the University by Royal Charter. He did, however, criticise the tri-partite relationship and was uncomfortable with its use as a "test" in all cases. Conversely, in *Joobeen*, Lord Prosser held that the University was entitled to expel a student for non-payment of fees since this was in essence a contractual relationship and not subject to judicial review.

Due to such confusion, the test has subsequently evolved today into an indicator of the competency of proceedings only in relation to particular disputes concerning contracts and employment matters. It is by no means a test which should be applied in all cases of judicial review and is certainly not a judicial "hurdle".

TITLE AND INTEREST TO SUE

It is a general principle of Scots law that a litigant must satisfy the Court of Session not only that they are the proper person to pursue the particular proceedings (*entitled*), but also that they have sufficient *interest* in the outcome of the proceedings. If an applicant fails to satisfy the court, this means that there is no dispute between the parties which is capable of being settled by judicial review. The question of title and interest is a separate and logically prior question which must be settled before a case proceeds. The concept was succinctly framed by Lord Dunedin in *D & J Nicol* v *Dundee Harbour Trs* (1915): "… I think it may fairly be said that for a person to have such a title, he must be a party (using the word in the widest sense) to some legal relation which gives him some right which the person against whom he raises the action either infringes or denies."

In that case, the pursuers were held to have title, not only as harbour ratepayers, but also as electors of the trustees by virtue of Act of Parliament. Similarly, in *Black* v *Tennant* (1899) Lord Guest held that neighbouring proprietors had title to sue to reduce an invalid grant of a public house licence since they had a statutory right to object to the licensing board on the grant of a licence. Thus it is clear that title to sue can be created through a statutory relationship. However, where a statute is drawn more specifically, those persons outside its scope will be denied title to sue despite having a sufficient interest, as in *Glasgow Rape Crisis Centre* v *Home Secretary* (2000) where it was held that the Crisis Centre had no title to sue since the decision of awarding a convicted rapist an entry visa was a matter solely between the Home Secretary and the applicant.

In cases where there is no direct statutory relationship, title to sue can often be based upon a common public right known as an *actio popularis*. This is based upon the principle that some rights are of such a public nature that any member of the public may have title and interest to enforce them. *Actio popularis* has applied in relation to public rights of way (*Jenkins* v *Robertson* (1867)) and rights to use land for recreation (*Home* v *Young* (1846)). How far public interest extends, however, has been doubted in the case of *Wilson* v *IBA* (1979) which dealt with the issue of television viewers and electors having the right to enforce a duty against the IBA when it had failed to be politically impartial during a referendum. The question left unanswered in this case was whether any member of the public should have title to sue, or whether a more direct or personal involvement would have to be shown.

The concept of sufficient interest was expounded by Lord Inglis in *Strang* v *Stewart* (1864) as: "... if there be a pecuniary or a patrimonial interest, however small, depending on the determination of the question, the parties have the right to involve the aid of a court of law to resolve their difference." However, the Court has moved away from an insistence on the presence of pecuniary interest and, provided that there is title, interest need be neither pecuniary nor large (*Gunstone* v *Scottish Women's Amateur Athletic Association* (1987)).

Whether a "pressure group" has sufficient interest in the pursuance of the rights of a member of the public has been doubtful under Scots law. In the leading case of *Scottish Old People's Welfare Council, Petrs* (1987), Age Concern Scotland, on behalf of the elderly, challenged the legality of a government circular which issued guidance on extra payments for severe weather conditions. It was held by Lord Clyde that the interest of the petitioners was too remote. Age Concern was an organisation furthering the interests of elderly people but its own membership did not consist of potential claimants who would directly benefit from a favourable decision. This is a markedly different stance from that in England and Wales, where pressure groups regularly petition for review on behalf of members of the public (*R* v *Secretary of State for Trade and Industry, ex parte Greenpeace Ltd* (1998)). Thus, the approach of having sufficient interest in Scotland can often place litigants at a disadvantage. In practice, pressure groups have always been able to fund and provide the means for an individual to raise a petition in Scotland, even if they do not front the actual case.

SUBSTANTIVE GROUNDS OF CHALLENGE

The law relating to the grounds of challenge for judicial review is ever evolving. This is because the law is based almost wholly upon precedent, with very little legislative input. This has allowed the law to develop in a flexible manner, dealing with each case based upon its own unique circumstances. The grounds of challenge have been developed by the courts over many years; however, the most modern authoritative statement on the grounds can be found in the decision of *Council of Civil Service Unions* v *Minister for Civil Service* (1985). In that case, Lord Diplock set out his famous catalogue of grounds of challenge: "... one can conveniently classify under three heads the grounds on which administrative action is subject to control by judicial review. The first ground I would call 'illegality', the second 'irrationality', and the third 'procedural impropriety'." In creating these categories, Lord Diplock did not intend them to be interpreted rigidly. He stated that they would be subject to future expansion and, indeed, he already spoke at this stage about the introduction of a possible fourth ground of challenge in the European principle of "proportionality".

Illegality

Almost all the powers and duties which public bodies possess are statutory, conferred by Act of Parliament or statutory instrument. So the limits of public powers and the extent of public duties are those which statute imposes or grants. Illegality is a central principle of administrative law and can be stated quite simply: a person or body acting under statutory powers can do only those things which statute permits. If a public body exercises its powers without statutory authorisation, then that action will be illegal or *ultra vires* (beyond the powers). The *ultra vires* doctrine is clearly illustrated in *McColl* v *Strathclyde RC* (1983) where the council was held to have acted *ultra vires* in attempting to add fluoride to the public water supply. The statutory powers of the council in this area came from the Water (Scotland) Act 1980 which allowed local authorities to provide a "wholesome" water supply. Since the fluoride was to be added to improve dental health, and not for wholesomeness, the actions were illegal.

There are a number of other aspects of illegality which are different from the simple application of *ultra vires*. Each of these must be examined in some detail in order to gain a fuller understanding of illegality as a ground of challenge.

Error of law

There is a difference between Scots law and English law in the matter of error of law. In England, it is a ground of challenge that an administrative body has made an error of law; however, in Scotland, this is not the case. The court can intervene and quash a decision only if it is *ultra vires*. However, if an administrative body acts within the remit of its powers, but in doing so has only made an error of law, then it has made an error of law *within* its jurisdiction. In such a case, the Scottish courts have no power to intervene. The reasoning for this is that if Parliament has given a body power to deal with certain matters, according to theory, Parliament must have intended that the statutory body should have the power to make not only legally correct decisions, but also decisions which go wrong in law.

The leading case is *Watt v Lord Advocate* (1979) where a man had been laid off work for 3 weeks following a work to rule in which he had not participated. The question to be decided was whether he was "directly interested" in the industrial action. If he was, he would not be entitled to unemployment benefit. The case went to the National Insurance Commissioner who decided Watt was directly interested. In the Outer House of the Court of Session, Lord Dunpark refused to intervene, concluding that the decision was within the Commissioner's power, even if it was wrong in law. On a further appeal, however, the Inner House overturned the decision, holding that the question raised a point of law and that the National Insurance Commissioner had stepped outside his power and acted *ultra vires*. He had not merely misinterpreted the law in attempting to answer the right question: he had, in fact, asked the wrong question.

Thus, in Scotland, if a body makes an error of law which is not *ultra vires*, the Court of Session will not be able to correct the error. The lack of a remedy is not, however, as important as it might seem, for two reasons. First, from many tribunals and statutory bodies, there is an appeal to the courts provided by statute on a question of law. Second, the courts are likely, as the *Watt* decision perhaps illustrates, to say that any serious error of law takes the decision-making body outwith its power.

Relevant considerations

When an administrative body is entrusted with a power, it is implicit that the power must be exercised taking into account all relevant considerations and excluding irrelevant ones. To say what factors are relevant in any particular case can be difficult, especially when the factors are not expressly laid down in statute. Thus, each case must be judged on its own circumstances.

In *Roberts* v *Hopwood* (1925), a political decision on sex equality was held to be an irrelevant consideration. Poplar Borough Council had the power to pay its employees "such wages as the council think fit". It decided to pay £4 a week to all employees (including females), which was substantially more than the national average. The District Auditor disallowed this as being contrary to law. On appeal, the House of Lords held that the council had been guided by irrelevant considerations and had used its power for an improper purpose, ie to achieve equality in wages. It had not allowed itself to be guided by relevant considerations such as the cost of living, and wages paid by national bodies and other local authorities.

In *Macfarlane* v *Glasgow Licensing Board* (1971), the Betting, Gaming and Lotteries Act 1963 stated that a licensing authority could refuse to renew a betting licence on the ground that premises had not been properly conducted. Schedule 4 to the 1963 Act continued to illustrate what constituted proper conduct. In this case, a customer had been refused payment of winnings because the bookmaker had lost the betting slip and so an objection to the renewal of the licence was lodged. Based upon the objection, the local authority refused renewal. It was held by the sheriff that the non-payment was an irrelevant consideration. It was not one of the matters relating to proper conduct specified in the statute. The Act made clear that relevant considerations were issues such as allowing under-age persons on the premises and restrictions on showing television, none of which had been considered.

A final example of irrelevant considerations can be seen in *R* v *Ealing LBC, ex parte Times Newspapers* (1986) where the publishers of *The Times* were involved in a bitter industrial dispute with former employees. In response to a call by the trade unions involved, Ealing Council barred from its libraries all copies of newspapers published by Times Newspapers Ltd. These publications had been part of the library service prior to the ban. The court held that the reason for the ban was that it could be used as a weapon in an industrial dispute. It was therefore not within the council's powers relating to libraries, and the dispute was an irrelevant consideration.

Improper purpose

A principle of the use of statutory powers is that they must be used for the purpose for which they are granted. This concept is closely related to that of relevant considerations. In *Rossi* v *Edinburgh Corp* (1903), ice-cream sellers had to be licensed under statute by the corporation. The statute in question made it an offence to sell ice-cream outside the hours of 8 am and 11 pm. The corporation proposed to insert clauses into the licences to the effect that the premises to which the licence related should not be kept open before 8 am or after 11 pm. The House of Lords held that the clauses were *ultra vires* since the statute did not give the corporation the power to regulate the opening of shops, only the sale of ice-cream.

Similarly, in *Chertsey UDC v Mixnam's Properties Ltd* (1964), under the Caravan Sites and Control of Development Act 1964, the council was responsible for licensing caravan sites. It was empowered to impose such conditions as it thought necessary or desirable on the occupier of the land. The council issued a licence subject to conditions that caravan occupiers should have security of tenure, that there was to be no restriction on the caravaners as to from whom they might buy goods, or on the formation of a tenants' association. All the conditions were subsequently held to be *ultra vires* since the Act was concerned with the licensing of land as a caravan site, and so it permitted conditions which related to the use of the site. It did not permit conditions which attempted to regulate the contracts between the site operator and the caravan occupants.

Improper delegation

The courts hold a presumption that a person or body entrusted with a power should not sub-delegate the exercise of the power to another. This principle is embodied in the Latin maxim *delegatus non potest delegare* – a delegate does not have the power to sub-delegate. This principle is not absolute, however, and delegation may be possible in certain circumstances. In *Vine v National Dock Labour Board* (1957), the House of Lords held that, in deciding whether a power to delegate is lawful, one has to consider the nature of the duty in question and the character of the person on whom it is put. In the case of an exercise of disciplinary powers, the House was clear that they could not be delegated.

It is accepted that where powers are granted to a Government Minister, they may be validly exercised by officials of the Minister's department. Only when a statute expressly states that a power must be exercised personally will sub-delegation be unlawful (*Lavender & Son v Minister for Housing and Local Government* (1970)).

Fettering discretion

Often, questions can arise as to whether a public authority can limit or restrict the exercise of its own powers – in effect, decide that it is not going to exercise its powers. This is known as fettering discretion and may be unlawful.

(1) By a self-imposed rule

Authorities which have a statutory discretion to do something are entitled to adopt a policy by which the exercise of the discretion will in future be determined. But a body given discretion must not completely disable itself from exercising that discretion. In the leading case of *R v Port of London Authority, ex parte Kynoch* (1919), the authority had a statutory power to construct docks. Other bodies were also empowered to apply to the authority for a licence to construct docks. The authority adopted the policy of not granting a licence for something which was within its own statutory powers of provision and so Kynoch was refused a licence. Lord Justice Bankes held that if a body had passed a rule or come to a decision not to hear any application of a particular nature, no matter who makes it, then this was unlawful. The authority was refusing to exercise a power given to it by Parliament, a power which Parliament must have intended it to use. If, on the other hand, a public body, in the exercise of its discretion, has adopted a general policy but is prepared to consider an application which is contrary to the policy and tells the applicant what the policy is, then, after hearing the application and considering it, it may refuse the application. In such circumstances the exercise of discretion is not wholly excluded even though there is a strong disposition to decide in accordance with the policy.

In *R v Criminal Injuries Compensation Board, ex parte RJC* (1978), the Compensation Board rejected an application based upon the self-imposed rule that a member of a gang injured in a gang fight would not receive an award. This decision was invalidated since, by applying that rule, the Board had fettered its discretion and disabled itself from considering on its merits the application of such a gang member, whereas the scheme required every case to be decided on its own merits.

(2) By agreement or contract

It is clear that an administrative body on which a power is conferred by statute or by common law cannot disable itself, by agreement or contract, from exercising that power. The leading authority in this area is *Ayr Harbour Trs v Oswald* (1883). Under the Ayr Harbour Act 1879, the Harbour Trustees had power to acquire land and could use such land for the erection of buildings, among other things. They entered into an agreement with the former owner of a piece of land that they would not obstruct his use of it for access to the harbour, ie they would not erect buildings or otherwise restrict his access. This contract was held to be *ultra vires* in that it fettered their future power to build on that particular land. The power had been conferred by Parliament for the public good and the right to exercise that power should not be restricted in any way.

Similarly, in *Stringer* v *Minister for Housing and Local Government* (1971), Cheshire County Council made an agreement with Manchester University that it would not permit development which would interfere with the operation of the university's telescope at Jodrell Bank. However, the Town and Country Planning Act 1962 stated that, in considering any application for planning permission, the planning authority had to take into account all material considerations, ie relevant factors. The council subsequently received an application to build in the area and refused it on the basis of the agreement. It was held that the authority had disabled itself from taking account of all the relevant factors and that the agreement was therefore *ultra vires*.

Irrationality and proportionality

Irrationality, as Lord Diplock expressed in the *Council of Civil Service Unions* case, is to be understood as *Wednesbury* unreasonableness. The concept of *Wednesbury* unreasonableness emanates from the celebrated case of *Associated Provincial Picture Houses Ltd* v *Wednesbury Corp* (1948) which did not purport to create new law but consolidated some already established points. In *Wednesbury*, the corporation had a statutory power to permit Sunday openings of cinemas "subject to such conditions as the authority thinks fit to impose". Wednesbury gave the plaintiff permission to open, subject to the condition that no children under 15 should be admitted, even if accompanied by an adult. The plaintiff sought a declaration from the court that the condition was *ultra vires*. In his judgment, Lord Greene emphasised two points: that the statute had given local authorities an unlimited power to impose conditions, and that it did not provide an appeal from the authority's decision on any ground. He then went on to consider to what extent the decision might be said to be "unreasonable":

> "... there may be something so absurd that no sensible person could ever dream that it lay within the powers of the authority. Warrington LJ in *Short* v *Poole Corporation* gave the example of the red-haired teacher, dismissed because she had red hair. That is unreasonable in one sense. In another sense it is taking into consideration extraneous matters. It is so unreasonable that it might almost be described as being done in bad faith; and in fact all these things run into one another."

In *Wednesbury*, it was quite clear that the subject-matter dealt with by the condition was a matter a reasonable authority would be justified in considering when deciding what condition to attach to the licence.

Indeed, the plaintiff did not argue that the council had taken an irrelevant matter into account, but that the decision was unreasonable, treating that as an independent ground of challenge. Lord Greene said that even where an authority has observed the relevancy rules, a decision may still be unreasonable when the authority has come to a conclusion so unreasonable that no reasonable decision-maker could ever come to it. However, the threshold of unreasonableness necessary to warrant judicial intervention was, and still is to some extent, pitched at an exceptionally high level. Thus, in returning to the facts before him, Lord Greene said that to prove a case of that kind would require something overwhelming and, in the case of Wednesbury, the facts did not come anywhere near the threshold level.

This unusually high threshold reflects the traditional reluctance of the courts to involve themselves in questioning the merits of discretionary decision-making. Indeed, given the constitutional position of the courts, a judge is on dangerous ground in striking down as unreasonable the decision of a statutory authority on a matter given to it for decision by Act of Parliament. This creates a situation whereby the judge substitutes his view on the merits for that of the authority, leading inevitably to claims of "*gouvernement des juges*".

However, with the arrival of the Human Rights Act 1998, the concept of unreasonableness has undergone a degree of adjustment. In the *Council of Civil Service Unions* case, Lord Diplock referred to the possible acceptance of proportionality into UK law. At this time, proportionality was well established in the jurisprudence of mainland Europe and, although absent as a separate ground of challenge under judicial review in the UK, elements of it could be traced in many decisions (*Roberts* v *Hopwood* (1925); and *R* v *Barnsley MBC, ex parte Hook* (1976)). In *R* v *Ministry of Defence, ex parte Smith* (1996), Lord Bingham stated that: "... in judging whether the decision maker has exceeded this margin of appreciation, the human rights context is important. The more substantial the interference with human rights, the more the court will require by way of justification before it is satisfied that the decisions are reasonable ...".

Thus, the European principle of proportionality has begun to alter the way in which unreasonableness is dealt with by the courts. The introduction of proportionality provides a more rigorous approach to judicial review and involves the court examining the relationship between administrative means and ends. It must examine the level of weight attached by the decision-maker to specific rights and considerations and assess whether the correct balance has been struck. In essence, proportionality is a much less subjective test than that of unreasonableness and attempts to soften the high threshold.

Proportionality should, however, be viewed with caution, since it has not replaced the *Wednesbury* standard of unreasonableness but has merely resulted in an adjustment to the law. The test of proportionality is only engaged in cases where Convention and fundamental rights are involved – in all other circumstances, the domestic law remains the same (*R (Association of British Civilian Internees – Far Eastern Region)* v *Secretary of State for Defence* (2003)). Thus, the concept of proportionality has been incorporated into *Wednesbury* unreasonableness but, for the time being, has not replaced it.

Procedural impropriety

In its strict sense, this is a different aspect of *ultra vires* and involves situations where there has been a failure to follow prescribed procedures. This is known as procedural *ultra vires*. However, in a broader sense, procedural impropriety incorporates the rules of natural justice, ie the rule against bias, and the right to a fair hearing. When there has been breach of the rules of natural justice then the courts may interfere with a decision based upon procedural impropriety. The concept of natural justice is dealt with in the following chapter of this book, therefore this section is restricted to an examination of procedural *ultra vires*.

Legislation relating to the activities of public bodies specifies a great number of procedural requirements. It covers such things as time limits for the service of notices, rights of appeal, and the giving of reasons for decisions, among many others. Where statute lays down statutory requirements, it does not generally specify the consequences that follow from non-compliance, ie it does not generally say whether failure to comply with the legislative procedures invalidates the action or not. Thus, it is almost entirely up to the courts in each case to decide on the issue. However, the courts have shown themselves reluctant to lay down firm rules on this matter and consequently the law has become somewhat fragmented. For example, the fact that a statute uses the word "shall" in relation to certain statutory requirements does not necessarily mean that failure to follow procedure necessarily invalidates the action. Broadly, the courts have to decide whether the requirements are *mandatory* and must be followed, otherwise the action will be invalidated; or *directive*, where failure to follow does not automatically invalidate.

However, this distinction has not been without difficulty and in *London and Clydeside Estates* v *Aberdeen DC* (1980), the distinction was held to be too prescriptive by Lord Hailsham who stressed the importance of dealing with each procedural requirement on a case-by-case-basis. Consequently, it is difficult to forecast how the courts will treat a particular requirement, but a few generalisations may be made:

(1) if an administrative requirement imposes some financial burden on a citizen, it is likely that the requirement is mandatory and must be strictly complied with (*Moss Empires* v *Assessor for Glasgow* (1917));

(2) if a failure in procedure has an adverse effect on a person's property rights, it is likely that the adherence to the procedure is mandatory (*Eldon Garages Ltd* v *Kingston-upon-Hull CBC* (1974));

(3) a failure to comply with a requirement to make an investigation or to carry out a consultation before making a decision that may affect a citizen is likely to invalidate any decision (*Grunwick Processing Laboratories Ltd* v *ACAS* (1978));

(4) where there is a duty to consult, a failure to give those consulted an adequate opportunity to express their views is likely to invalidate a decision (*Lee* v *Secretary of State for Education and Science* (1968)); and

(5) where a statute gives a right of appeal against a decision, procedures for informing citizens of that right are likely to be mandatory (*London and Clydeside Estates* v *Aberdeen DC* (1980)).

REMEDIES

Under Scots law, the three most important remedies are reduction, declarator and interdict. Each of these remedies has been long established, however, a new, simplified procedure for their use came into force in 1985, following the recommendations of the Dunpark Committee. Where an application for exercise of the court's supervisory jurisdiction is made, the court may make such order in relation to the offending decision as it sees fit, whether or not such an order was sought in the application; in other words, an application will not fail if it covers one specific remedy but it should have specified another. If appropriate, the correct remedy will be granted. The Court of Session is reasonably flexible, and all three remedies may be sought in the same case, as well as damages.

Reduction

Utilising this remedy, the court may rescind, quash or set aside any written document, including the decision of an inferior court, tribunal or other public body. The grounds of reduction include all grounds which may render the document *ultra vires* (*Palmer* v *Inverness Hospitals Board* (1963)). Reduction is a very general remedy, but there are a few limitations placed upon its use:

(a) a dismissed employee cannot seek reduction of a notice of dismissal;

(b) reduction will not be permitted if a lesser remedy will suffice (*British Oxygen Co* v *South-West Scotland Electricity Board* (1956));

(c) reduction is a negative remedy in that another decision cannot be substituted in its place by the court; and

(d) reduction will not be granted if there will be no effect on the position of the parties by virtue of the action (*Shetland Line* v *Secretary of State for Scotland* (1996)).

A person may seek partial reduction of a decision or part of a document, for example that a condition attached to a licence is *ultra vires*. Partial reduction will only be considered when the offending parts of a document or decision can be appropriately severed from the remainder. In *Darney* v *Calder DC* (1904), a firm of glue manufacturers sought to set up a business in an area where glue production was considered an "offensive business"; thus, they obtained a conditional licence. The firm sought reduction of this condition as being *ultra vires*, but it was held that the condition was an inseparable part of the licence, so reduction was incompetent.

Declarator

The issue of a declarator involves the court declaring the existence of a right. This can be a right of any kind, for example a question of status, and is not entirely confined to administrative law. It can be obtained in either the Court of Session or the sheriff court, although it should be noted that the sheriff court cannot grant a declarator relating to administrative law matters (*Brown* v *Hamilton DC* (1983)).

The courts will not grant a declarator to settle hypothetical or abstract questions, nor any power entrusted by statute to the exclusive jurisdiction of a specialised tribunal. It may, however, be sought where some future right is in dispute. In *Rossi* v *Edinburgh Corp* (1904), Rossi sought a declarator that a proposed licence should not contain prohibitory conditions, such as not selling ice-cream on Sundays. The corporation had not yet tried to enforce the terms of the licence. Rossi could have waited until then, but he chose to take action early, to prevent enforcement of the licence; thus, a future right was being disputed. The court issued the declarator he sought, namely that to grant a licence subject to such conditions would be *ultra vires*.

However, a declarator will not be granted where it can have no practical effect in settling a dispute. In *Smith & Griffin* v *Lord Advocate* (1950), the court refused to grant a declarator that Griffin had been a member of the Navy, since the issue in dispute was whether he was entitled to a pension. The court could not grant a declarator because Griffin's pension entitlement was, by virtue of legislation, a matter subject to ministerial decision. Thus, the matter was not within the jurisdiction of the court.

Normally, a declarator is accompanied by an action for enforcement of the right declared. In *Baker* v *Glasgow DC* (1981), Baker sought a declarator in order to question the legality of a condition in a taxi licence. He also sought an interdict to have the council ordered not to impose the condition.

Interdict

The purpose of an interdict is to prevent injury to or infringement of any right. It is an order of the court prohibiting the implementation of a decision or the continuance of an action and can be sought in a variety of circumstances, for example to prevent the establishing of a local authority printing service (*Graham* v *Glasgow Corp* (1936)); to prevent a local authority supporting a political publication (*Meek* v *Lothian RC* (1983)); and to prevent fluoridation of the public water supply (*McColl* v *Strathclyde RC* (1983)).

When judicial proceedings are pending, an interim interdict may be granted to maintain the *status quo* until the outcome of those proceedings is known. Whether or not interim interdict is granted will depend on the balance of convenience. In *Innes* v *Royal Burgh of Kirkcaldy* (1963), the proposal of the Royal Burgh to reduce council house rents by one-quarter was challenged. The court held that the balance of convenience lay in maintaining the existing level of rents, from the point of view that if the reduction was found to be unlawful, tenants would possibly have to find large sums of money to repay the debt.

Interdict is a discretionary remedy. It may be refused even where a proposed action is of doubtful legality, or if there is another competent remedy, such as a statutory penalty or a statutory means of redress. A long delay in taking action or apparent acquiescence in a particular action may lead to an interdict being refused. Interdict may also be excluded when legislation has laid down a system of enforcement, including penalties for breach (*Magistrates of Buckhaven and Methil* v *Wemyss Coal Co* (1932)).

Remedies provided by statute

When Parliament confers powers and duties upon public authorities, it often also provides special procedures for enforcement or appeals or adjudication of disputes. In general, where there is some statutory means of challenging a decision, the Court of Session will require an applicant to resort to that procedure before seeking a remedy; otherwise an action will be dismissed as premature (*Nahar* v *Strathclyde RC* (1986)). The adoption of this rule is embodied in the principle that the court should not seek to exercise the discretion of another authority or upset the statutory framework for enforcing the law.

The statutory procedures which exist are numerous and there are too many to list definitively. However, examples would include:

(a) the right of appeal by an applicant to the Scottish Ministers on the refusal of a planning permission;

(b) confirmation of local authority byelaws by the Scottish Ministers;

(c) the exercise of a sheriff's powers relating to licensing appeals; and

(d) an appeal from a tribunal to a superior tribunal, such as from an employment tribunal to the Employment Appeals Tribunal.

Essential Facts

- Judicial review is an inherent common law power of the Court of Session in Scotland.
- The judicial review process is confined to whether an administrative body's decision is wrong in *law*, not with its *merits*.
- The competency of an application for review in Scotland does not depend upon any distinction between public law and private law.
- A potential litigant must satisfy the Court of Session that he has title and interest to sue; if an applicant fails to satisfy the court, this means that there is no dispute which is capable of being settled by judicial review.
- The substantive grounds of challenge under judicial review are illegality; irrationality (or unreasonableness); procedural impropriety; and, more recently, proportionality.
- The most common remedies sought under judicial review are reduction, declarator, and interdict.

Essential Cases

Moss Empires v Assessor for Glasgow (1917): definition of the supervisory jurisdiction.

Guthrie v Miller (1827): the distinction between law, facts and merits.

West v Secretary of State for Scotland (1992): the scope of judicial review; clarification of public/private law distinction.

Scottish Old People's Welfare Council, Petrs (1987): an outline of title and interest to sue.

Council of Civil Service Unions v Minister for Civil Service (1985): an outline of the substantive grounds of challenge under judicial review; the Diplock catalogue.

McColl v Strathclyde RC (1983): an example of an action of an administrative body being declared *ultra vires*.

Associated Provincial Picture Houses Ltd v Wednesbury Corp (1948): an explanation of "unreasonableness" and the creation of the high-threshold "*Wednesbury*"-style unreasonableness.

11 PARLIAMENTARY OMBUDSMEN

PARLIAMENTARY COMMISSIONER FOR ADMINISTRATION

Introduction

Since the early 19th century, Scandinavian countries have had an official, known as the Ombudsman, whose function is to investigate the grievances of ordinary citizens. The word "ombudsman" itself is Norse in origin and means "commissioner". The appointment of such a commissioner in the United Kingdom is comparatively recent, dating from the Parliamentary Commissioner for Administration Act 1967. Previously, complaints against government departments would be pursued either by complaining to an MP or by seeking judicial review. Both of these mechanisms are, of course, limited since MPs cannot mount a very effective investigation into the working of government departments, and largely have to limit themselves to asking questions of Ministers in the House of Commons, while judicial review can only be invoked by those with title and interest to sue and is limited to reviewing the legality of the actions.

To address these issues, the Whyatt Report on *The Citizen and Administration* (1961) advocated the creation of an Ombudsman as adopted in the Scandinavian countries. The primary aim of the Ombudsman would be to investigate complaints of maladministration in central government departments. Despite considerable opposition to the concept, the Ombudsman was created by virtue of the Parliamentary Commissioner for Administration Act 1967.

Constitution, appointment and tenure

The Parliamentary Commissioner for Administration Act 1967 establishes the office of Parliamentary Commissioner for Administration (PCA), commonly known as the Westminster Ombudsman. The independence of the PCA from the Executive is protected and the 1967 Act affords a degree of security of tenure. The PCA is appointed by the Crown on the advice of the Prime Minister and holds office during good behaviour subject to a power of removal on address from both Houses of Parliament. Thus, the tenure is similar to that of a High Court judge. The PCA also has a salary fixed by statute; it is chargeable to the Consolidated Fund and carries its own staff, subject to Treasury approval as to numbers and conditions of service.

Jurisdiction

The primary function of the PCA is to investigate complaints by private citizens that they have suffered injustice as a result of maladministration by government departments, agencies and non-departmental bodies. The full list of bodies subject to the jurisdiction of the PCA is listed in Sch 2 to the 1967 Act and includes all major government departments as well as other non-departmental bodies such as the Arts Council and the Equal Opportunities Commission. As regards those departments subject to investigation, the PCA cannot investigate complaints relating to the exercise of legislative functions, such as the preparation or creation of delegated legislation, although he can investigate complaints into the way in which a scheme set up by way of delegated legislation is actually being administered.

There are also a number of areas which are outwith the Ombudsman's jurisdiction. These can be found in Sch 3 to the 1967 Act and include, *inter alia*, matters certified by a Secretary of State to affect relations between the UK Government and any other Government or international organisation; the commencement of civil or criminal proceedings before any court of law in the UK; action taken in matters relating to contractual or other commercial transactions of government; and action taken in respect of any personnel matters. The Act also states that the PCA may not investigate a matter where the citizen generally has a right of redress before any tribunal or court.

As mentioned above, the Ombudsman can only investigate instances of maladministration causing injustice. However, the term "maladministration" is not defined anywhere within the 1967 Act. This has often been criticised by observers of the system. However, this was a deliberate act of the legislature and has allowed the concept to develop unrestricted, on a case-by-case basis. In the Second Reading debate on the Bill preceding the 1967 Act, Richard Crossman MP famously catalogued possible examples of maladministration as bias, neglect, inattention, delay, incompetence, ineptitude, perversity, turpitude and arbitrariness. Its definition is wide and encompassing, however, it does not generally include the merits of a decision and there must always be an element of injustice present.

Making a complaint

The PCA cannot instigate an investigation personally but can only respond to complaints received from members of the public. Currently, the PCA is only entitled to investigate complaints made in writing by a Member of the House of Commons at the instance of a member of the public. The public have no direct access to the PCA and must first approach an MP and request that the complaint be forwarded in writing to the Commissioner. The MP may, of course, refuse. This is known as the "MP filter" and is intended to serve three functions. First, it acknowledges the status of the Commissioner as a servant of Parliament; second, it provides the MP with an opportunity to deal with the complaint as he sees fit; and, finally, it allows inappropriate and vexatious complaints to be rejected before reaching the PCA, thus reducing workload.

The MP filter has been much criticised and the UK and France are the only two European countries which have such a filter. The arguments in favour of the MP are not particularly convincing and, in any event, most MPs have today adopted a policy of always referring complaints to the PCA, as they are reluctant to reject them for fear of appearing unhelpful to constituents. Thus, the filter provides no real practical purpose. The Parliamentary Commissioner (Amendment) Bill was introduced into the House of Commons on 15 February 2000, with the intention of removing the MP filter and allowing the PCA to investigate complaints received directly from members of the public. However, this was a Private Member's Bill and it failed to progress through Parliament. Given that the Scottish Parliamentary Ombudsman has no filter, it is likely that there will be a further attempt at abolition in the near future.

Complaints must also be made within 12 months of the date on which the citizen first had notice of the issue complained of. This is subject to a discretionary power to allow late applications in extraordinary circumstances.

Investigations

If a complaint does fall within the jurisdiction of the Commissioner, then an investigation may be conducted. At this primary stage, the PCA should try to promote an amicable settlement between the individual and the department or body concerned. However, if this is not possible then an investigation will proceed in accordance with the 1967 Act. All investigations are conducted in private, and the department or body complained of must be given an opportunity to comment on any allegations contained in the complaint. The PCA has powers similar to those of a High Court judge for securing the presence of witnesses and the production of documents, and Crown privilege or public interest immunity cannot be used to exempt information from investigation by the Commissioner.

The PCA is protected in the conducting of investigations by the laws relating to contempt of court and so any wilful obstruction of an investigation may be punished as if it were a contempt. Complainants and witnesses who have spent time in assisting an investigation are entitled to claim reasonable expenses.

Reports

On completing an investigation, the PCA must report the findings to the MP who originally referred the complaint, and to the department or body against whom the complaint was made. If the Commissioner finds that injustice was caused by maladministration and this has not been rectified then he may lay a special report before both Houses of Parliament. The Commissioner may also make other special reports as are necessary and must make an annual report to Parliament. The reports of the Commissioner and certain other information relating to investigations are absolutely privileged in the law of defamation.

Enforcement

The PCA cannot have any recommendations or reports enforced by law. The Commissioner has no executive power and cannot alter decisions made or order payment of compensation. If, after conducting an investigation, the Commissioner considers that an injustice has not or will not be remedied then he may lay before each House of Parliament a special report on the case, recommending remedial action. That is, however, the extent of the PCA's powers. The issue must then be left to the doctrine of ministerial responsibility, the assumption being that pressure will be put upon the Minister concerned to take remedial action. This may not seem like a particularly strong method of enforcement, however, in reality, there is strong pressure on the Government to comply with the PCA's findings. Such special powers are often not necessary, since an agreed settlement involving, for example, an apology or compensation may be reached between the aggrieved individual and the government department concerned.

Reform

Today, there is less in the way of criticism of the PCA and more in the way of concern about the workload of the Commissioner. Over the last decade or so, the PCA's total workload has increased from 801 complaints in 1991 to 4,189 complaints in 2005. Furthermore, up until 2002, the

Parliamentary Commissioner also held the offices of Scottish Parliamentary Commissioner for Administration, and Health Service Commissioner for England, Scotland, and Wales; a particularly burdensome remit, fuelling the rise in complaints.

The high instance of complaints would seem to suggest that the PCA is a highly successful and efficient body. However, the system has recently come under intense public and parliamentary scrutiny. Much of the criticism arising from this has not necessarily been directed solely at the PCA but more at the lack of uniformity across the Ombudsmen system. Besides the PCA, there are several other public- and private-sector ombudsmen in England and Wales, for example the Commissioner for Local Administration (dealing with local government), and the Legal Services Ombudsman. Each of these Ombudsmen has a separate remit, with differing powers and procedures, with the result that it can often be confusing for a citizen to know exactly where to direct complaints. Consequently, the Cabinet Office has published a review of the system, entitled *Review of the Public Sector Ombudsmen in England* (2000). This paper has been well received but it has yet to elicit any major legislative change. Among its key proposals, the paper suggests having a collegiate ombudsmen system, with a direct point of access for citizens. This would introduce a more uniform approach and would make the system more accessible at the point of use for aggrieved citizens. Such change would, however, have to take into account the already pressurised resources of the existing system.

SCOTTISH PUBLIC SERVICES OMBUDSMAN

Introduction

Ombudsman reform within Scotland has been a modern success story. Section 91 of the Scotland Act 1998 placed an obligation upon the Scottish Parliament to create an Ombudsman (or to make alternative arrangements) to deal with any complaints of maladministration in devolved areas. Thus, from July 1999 until 2002, complaints against the Scottish Executive, the Scottish Administration and other public bodies in Scotland were handled by the Westminster Ombudsman in his role as Scottish Parliamentary Commissioner for Administration. This interim period allowed the Scottish Parliament to hold a series of consultations in order to canvass opinion as to the best mechanism for handling complaints within Scotland.

The result of this consultation was the Scottish Public Services Ombudsman Act 2002 which has established a modern collegiate approach to complaint handling in Scotland. Under the 2002 Act, the various Scottish public-sector Ombudsmen have been amalgamated into one centralised body, allowing for ease of use and simplicity. Although the strengths of the separate Ombudsmen were widely recognised, the disparities among the offices were frequently confusing for members of the public. The new "one-stop-shop" approach allows the Ombudsman system to become more co-ordinated and centralised.

Constitution, appointment and tenure

Under the 2002 Act, the new Scottish Ombudsman has assumed the jurisdiction of the transitional post held by the PCA, although the PCA may still investigate maladministration within reserved areas of government. The Scottish Ombudsman has also assumed the jurisdiction of other pre-existing ombudsmen in Scotland, namely the Commissioner for Local Administration in Scotland, the Health Service Commissioner for Scotland, the Housing Association Ombudsman for Scotland, the External Adjudicators for Scottish Enterprise and Highlands and Islands Enterprise, and the Mental Welfare Commission.

The Scottish Ombudsman is appointed by the Queen on the nomination of the Scottish Parliament, and is assisted by three Deputy Ombudsmen who are similarly appointed. The Deputy Ombudsmen are intended to reflect the expertise held by former office holders and, to this end, the current Deputies are drawn from the fields of health, housing and local government.

The Ombudsman and any Deputy Ombudsman may hold office for a period not exceeding 5 years, subject to a power of removal in pursuance of a resolution of the Scottish Parliament. Office holders are eligible for re-appointment but may not serve a third consecutive term unless through special circumstances it is in the public interest for them to do so. In any event, any office holder who attains the age of 65 must vacate office on 31 December of that year.

The Ombudsman and any Deputy Ombudsman have a salary fixed by the Parliamentary Corporation and the office also carries its own staff, subject to approval as to numbers and conditions of service.

Jurisdiction

The primary role of the Scottish Ombudsman is to investigate complaints from members of the public who claim to have suffered injustice or hardship as a consequence of maladministration by the Scottish Government, agencies and other non-departmental bodies. Schedule 2 to the 2002 Act provides a full list of bodies subject to the jurisdiction of the Ombudsman and is split into two Parts. Part 1 contains a list of authorities which cannot be amended and includes members of the Scottish Executive, health service bodies, local authorities and the police, among others. Part 2 contains a list of Scottish public authorities, and cross-border public authorities, such as Scottish Enterprise, the Scottish Legal Aid Board and the National Consumer Council. This list may be amended in the future by Order in Council.

With regard to those bodies subject to investigation, there are a number of restrictions placed upon the jurisdiction of the Ombudsman. Schedule 4 to the 2002 Act excludes 15 categories of investigation; these include action taken for the prevention of crime, any civil or criminal legal proceedings, action taken which relates to contractual or commercial matters, and any decision made in a judicial capacity. Furthermore, the Ombudsman may not question the merits of discretionary decisions unless there has clearly been maladministration, nor may any matter be investigated where the complainant has an alternative remedy available, for example a right of appeal.

As with the PCA, the concept of maladministration has no direct statutory definition in order to allow flexibility. But there have been criticisms of the Scottish Ombudsman in that s 5 of the 2002 Act includes alongside maladministration the right to investigate "service failures" and "any action" (where the action is taken by a registered social landlord, or a health or family care provider). Thus, s 5 essentially provides additional grounds of investigation which are exercisable only in very specific circumstances. This is somewhat at odds with the centralised ethos of the 2002 Act and may add unwarranted confusion for users of the system. In response, the Scottish Parliament has defended the disparities, claiming that they are necessary to reflect the procedural nuances of the pre-existing Ombudsmen.

Making a complaint

An innovation of the 2002 Act can be found in the removal of the "MP filter" concept, resulting in the absence of an "MSP filter" for Scotland. Thus, in keeping with the spirit of a collegiate approach, citizens may complain directly to the Scottish Ombudsman. It is also possible to have a complaint lodged on a person's behalf by any authorised person, for example an MSP or a local councillor. As with the PCA, complaints must be made within 12 months of the date on which the citizen first had notice of the issue complained of, subject to a discretionary power to allow late applications in extraordinary circumstances.

Complaints may be submitted either in writing or electronically. This is a key difference from the procedure followed by the PCA, where all complaints must be submitted in writing. Although the vast majority of complaints are generally written, there is a growing sector of the public who prefer to deal with issues via the Internet. As a result, citizens may submit complaints using an electronic submission form available on the Ombudsman's website. The Ombudsman also has a discretionary power to accept oral complaints in extraordinary circumstances.

Investigations

If a complaint falls within the jurisdiction of the Ombudsman then an investigation may be conducted. The procedure for investigation is very similar to that of the PCA and is in fact modelled closely upon the 1967 Act. Investigations are conducted in private, and the department or body complained of must be given an opportunity to comment on any allegations contained in the complaint. The Ombudsman may compel the production of any information or documents required and has similar powers to that of a Court of Session judge for securing the presence and examination of witnesses. Crown privilege or public interest immunity claims cannot be used in relation to documents subject to investigation by the Ombudsman.

Reports

On completing an investigation, the Ombudsman must report the findings to the complainant – the department, body or person against whom the complaint was made, and the Scottish Ministers. Furthermore, a report must be laid before the Scottish Parliament which must not identify any person other than the department, body or person complained of. If the Ombudsman finds that hardship or injustice has been caused by maladministration and this has not been rectified, then a special report may be laid before the Parliament. In addition, the Ombudsman must also present an annual report to the Parliament.

Enforcement

As with the PCA, the Scottish Ombudsman cannot have any recommendations or reports enforced by law. The Ombudsman has no executive power and cannot alter decisions made or order payment of compensation. If, after conducting an investigation, the Ombudsman considers that an injustice has not or will not be remedied then a special report on the case is the strongest form of action. Enforcement is left up to ministerial responsibility and the assumption that pressure will be put upon the Government to take remedial action. This may not seem like a particularly strong method of enforcement for a modern Ombudsman system. However, the Scottish Executive identified that keeping enforcement powers to a minimum would in fact aid co-operation between bodies and the Scottish Ombudsman, whereas investing draconian powers of intervention would be likely to hinder investigations. To date, the Scottish Executive appears to have been correct and many cases have been settled through apology, compensation or remedial action stemming from the Ombudsman's comments.

FURTHER REFORM

The concept of maladministration

Maladministration has frequently been criticised as too narrow and can be contrasted with the remit of the New Zealand Ombudsman who may investigate any decision or act which appears to be "wrong". It was suggested by the 1977 Justice Report *Our Fettered Ombudsman* that "maladministration" be replaced with the phrase "unreasonable, unjust or oppressive", but this change has never materialised. Conversely, it can be argued that the concept of maladministration is not in fact narrow, and that it might well be possible to challenge unreasonable, unjust or oppressive actions by claiming that they are the result of ineptitude or arbitrariness on the part of government officials. A previous Commissioner, Sir Idwal Pugh, stated publicly that he regarded his work as being concerned with just such unreasonable, unjust or oppressive actions, and he would have no hesitation in concluding that there must have been some aspect of maladministration in the procedure leading to the taking of such a decision. The courts have not insisted that the complaint must indicate what aspects of maladministration are alleged. The application merely needs to indicate what the complaint is about, leaving it to the Ombudsman to discover any maladministration. This approach can be seen in *R v Local Commissioner for Administration for the North and East Area of England, ex parte Bradford City Council* (1979).

However, the concept of maladministration is certainly confusing. This is especially true of the work of the Scottish Ombudsman, where an investigation may go beyond maladministration into service failures and other actions, but only in limited circumstances. This may be likely to result in the less socially confident, and less articulate, being able to understand the nature of any complaint.

Inadequate use of press and publicity

It has often been stressed that the Ombudsmen should make more extensive use of the press, by supplying full details of all reports. Traditionally, reviews and comment upon the reports appear in various specialised journals but general public awareness of the system is low. Greater publication of reports would also bring extra pressure to bear on the Government to correct any injustice uncovered. To date, the Ombudsmen have not utilised any greatly increased amount of publicity, however, they have attempted to be more accessible and user-friendly. This has been achieved chiefly through information technology and the creation of user-friendly websites providing a portal for initial complainants. The website of the PCA can be accessed at www.ombudsman.org.uk, and that of the Scottish Ombudsman at www.scottishombudsman.org.uk.

Jurisdiction

The Ombudsmen cannot carry out an investigation where the act in question has been carried out in accordance with law and without maladministration. This is the case even though the law in question is operating in an unfair, unreasonable, oppressive or unintended way. Indeed, it may be that the fault is not with a government department or body but with the legislation that they are obliged to execute. The question thus arises as to whether Ombudsmen should be able to investigate such instances and have the power to suggest changes in legislation, including statutory instruments. This would be beneficial to Parliament since the Ombudsmen are ideally placed to form a view as to whether current legislation is working in an undesirable way "on the ground".

Essential Facts

- The Parliamentary Commissioner for Administration (PCA) was created by the Parliamentary Commissioner for Administration Act 1967 which lays out the composition, jurisdiction and powers of the PCA. The remit of the PCA extends to England and Wales, as well as any reserved matters for Scotland.

- The primary role of the PCA is to investigate complaints by private citizens who have suffered injustice as a result of maladministration by government departments, agencies and non-departmental bodies. Complaints must be made in writing and initially through an MP; this is known as the MP filter and has been much criticised.

- The office of the Scottish Public Services Ombudsman (SPSO) was created by the Scottish Public Services Ombudsman Act 2002 which lays out the composition, jurisdiction and powers of the SPSO.

- The SPSO is a collegiate body and also incorporates the jurisdiction of pre-existing ombudsmen in Scotland, namely the Commissioner for Local Administration in Scotland, the Health Service Commissioner for Scotland, the Housing Association Ombudsman for Scotland, the External Adjudicators for Scottish Enterprise and Highlands and Islands Enterprise, and the Mental Welfare Commission.

- The primary role of the SPSO is to investigate complaints from members of the public who have suffered injustice or hardship as a consequence of maladministration. Complaints may be made directly to the Ombudsman since there is no "MSP filter".

- Both the PCA and the SPSO have the power to conduct investigations into instances of maladministration and have statutory authority to compel the production of documents and witnesses.

- On completion of an investigation, the PCA must produce a report containing findings and recommendations and may lay a special report before Parliament where no remedial action is taken in light of the report. The SPSO must act similarly, with a special report being laid ultimately before the Scottish Parliament.

- Neither the PCA nor the SPSO has any legal powers of enforcement. They cannot coerce action to be taken in light of their recommendations. Instead, they rely upon co-operation from bodies complained of through ministerial responsibility and Government pressure.

INDEX